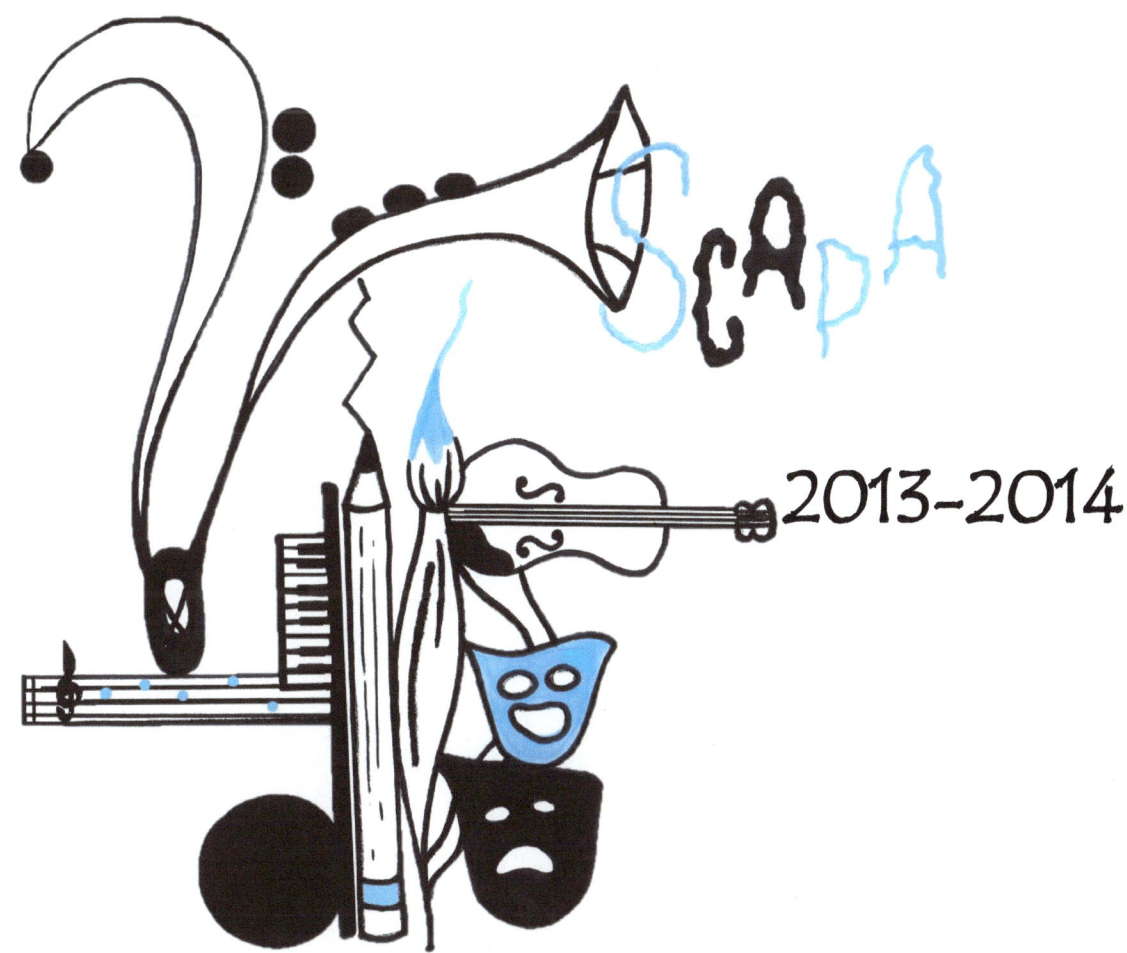

Literature and Art Magazine

Cover Art by Anna Gilligan

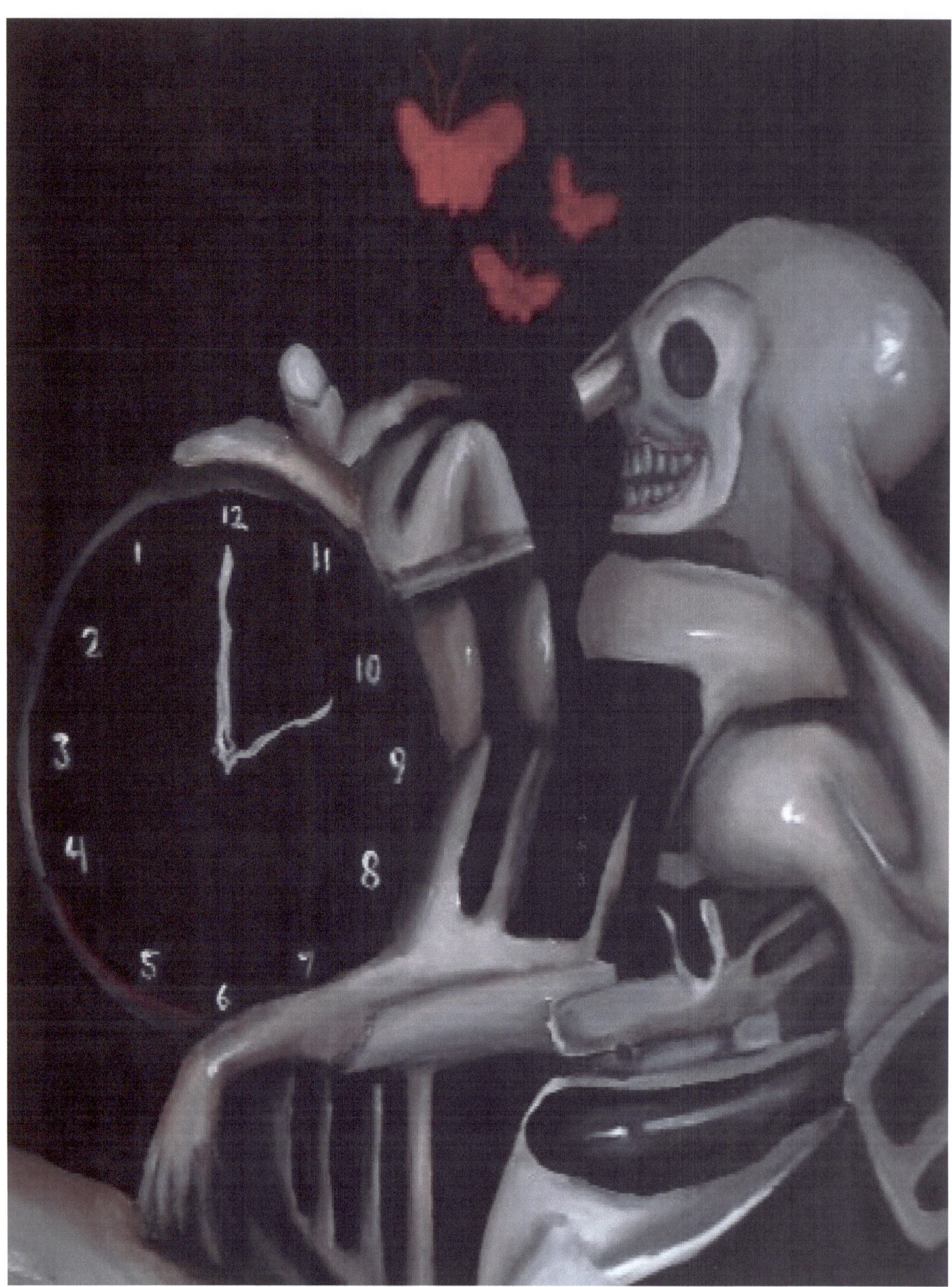

Illustrated by Brent Comely, 8

An Unfortunate Encounter

by **Avery Logsdon**, 8

H ad Dustin known about what he was getting into, when he shot into the woods like a panther, he wouldn't have gone. Had Dustin known what was lurking in the woods, he certainly would not have gone in. He probably would have stayed back in his house, duct-taped to a chair with a rifle overtop his soiled pants. Unfortunately, Dustin did not have ESP (unlike some in the forest) and thus, he took the dare, ultimately dooming himself to a life of madness.

It all started when Terry told him that he had seen some crazy things in the forest and that he'd give Dustin ten dollars to go in there. Dustin had, at first, been hesitant to do so, but the rush of adrenaline had pulled him in. Wearing only a light jacket and a muddy White Sox hat, Dustin ventured out into the night.

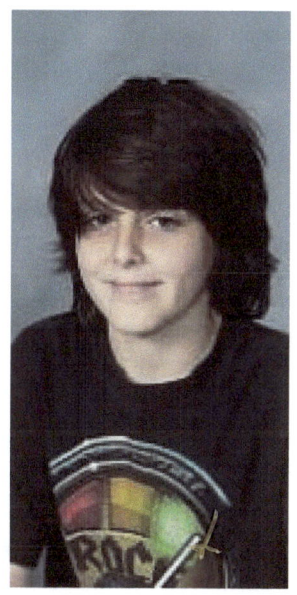

Avery Logsdon, 8
Creative Writing Major

When he was about a half mile into the woods, when the light of the small ramshackle house was still visible, Dustin considered going back. He didn't have a flashlight, and nothing he saw was exciting—other than two caterpillars mating, which he had chuckled at for a full six minutes.

Quietly, he turned around, careful not to look like a chicken, and started back towards the house, which was faint on the tree-dotted horizon. There was a discreet crack, and Dustin looked down, wondering if he had stepped on a stick or something. Suddenly, a creature pounced out in front of him, fangs bared, and it stormed over to him, tracking up mud and leaves behind it.

Dustin screamed and fell backwards onto the seat of his jeans. The ground was cold under him, and the creature didn't let up, as it edged forward. Dustin screamed again, tearing the left leg of his pants from the knee down, as he struggled to get up. There was a boom like a gunshot. Dustin jumped towards the ground, clutching onto the dirt with his grimy fingernails. The creature moved towards him slightly but then fled backwards, as the gunshots grew louder.

"Gus?" Came a confused voice.

"Terry?" Dustin said, ultimately fearing that whoever it was, was not Terry.

"Gus?" the voice said again.

"Terry?" said Dustin, trying to confirm that he was not Gus.

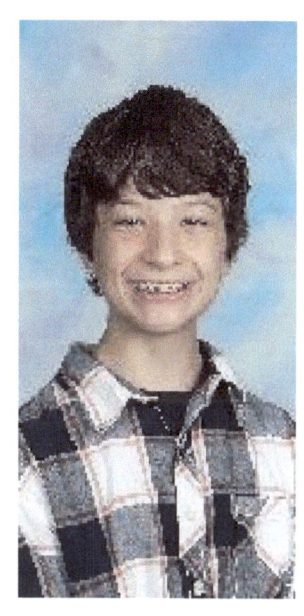

Brent Comely, 8
Art Major

"Gus?" the man asked again.

"Terry?" he said, trying to make his point.

"Gus?"

Dustin sighed. "Terry?" he asked again.

"Gus?"

"I'M NOT FREAKING GUS!"

"Oh." BLAM! There was another gunshot.

"What are you doing!?!" Dustin exclaimed.

"Gus?"

Dustin sighed. "Fine. Yes. I am Gus. Just don't shoot me."

A bearded man with orange hair, and an overly-large camouflage hat emerged from the bushes. "Say! You aren't Gus!" The man said. He fired his gun up again.

"No, stop! I'm not Gus! Don't shoot me!"

"What are you doing here, not Gus?"

"What are you doing here?" Dustin asked.

"I'm looking for a friend," the man replied.

"Gus, I presume," Dustin said, already turning around. "I'll be on my way now."

"Alone?" The man looked horrified. He started muttering to himself. "Well, if you're alone, then I'll be alone and then----" He looked up, his mouth gaping. "Just help me find Gus… please."

"I'm just gonna go," Dustin said, walking back to his house.

Suddenly, there was a roar and a shriek.

"What the heck?" Dustin turned and fell, the damp dirt seeping through his holey jeans.

There was another roar, and the man with the orange hair ran out from behind the over brush of trees.

"Go!" he yelled, "There's no time to waste!" Ironically, shortly after him saying that, he tripped over an uprooted root and did a somersault down a hill onto a bed of rocks.

"Owww!" he yelled.

"Come on!" Dustin grabbed the man's sweaty hand and tried to pull, but it was too late. He felt his hands go clammy, then he fell back onto the damp dirt once again. Something was over him, something that he had never seen before.

Directions

by Serena Male, 7

Upon that floor I stood,

Looking all around,

I see many things,

A rocky cliff,

A cloudy sky.

Sun is shining on the ocean,

Ships are leaving port,

Fishermen are pulling in their nets,

And farmers are plowing their fields.

There is snow on the mountains,

And glaciers to the North,

Icebergs floating through the sea,

And cool winds blowing through the hills,

Birds of all kind,

And tropics to the South,

Australia,

New Zealand,

And Singapore to the West.

The Pillars of Life,

Vega,

And Sirius A to the East.

There I stood upon that floor,

Looking all around me,

At the books of a library.

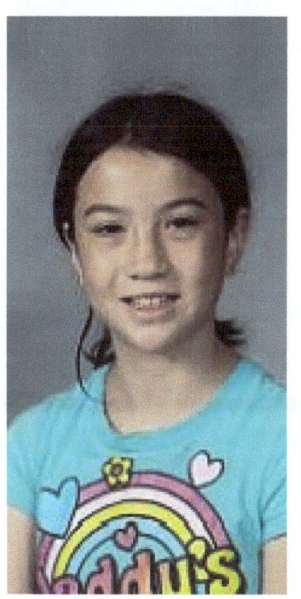

Serena Male, 7
Piano Major

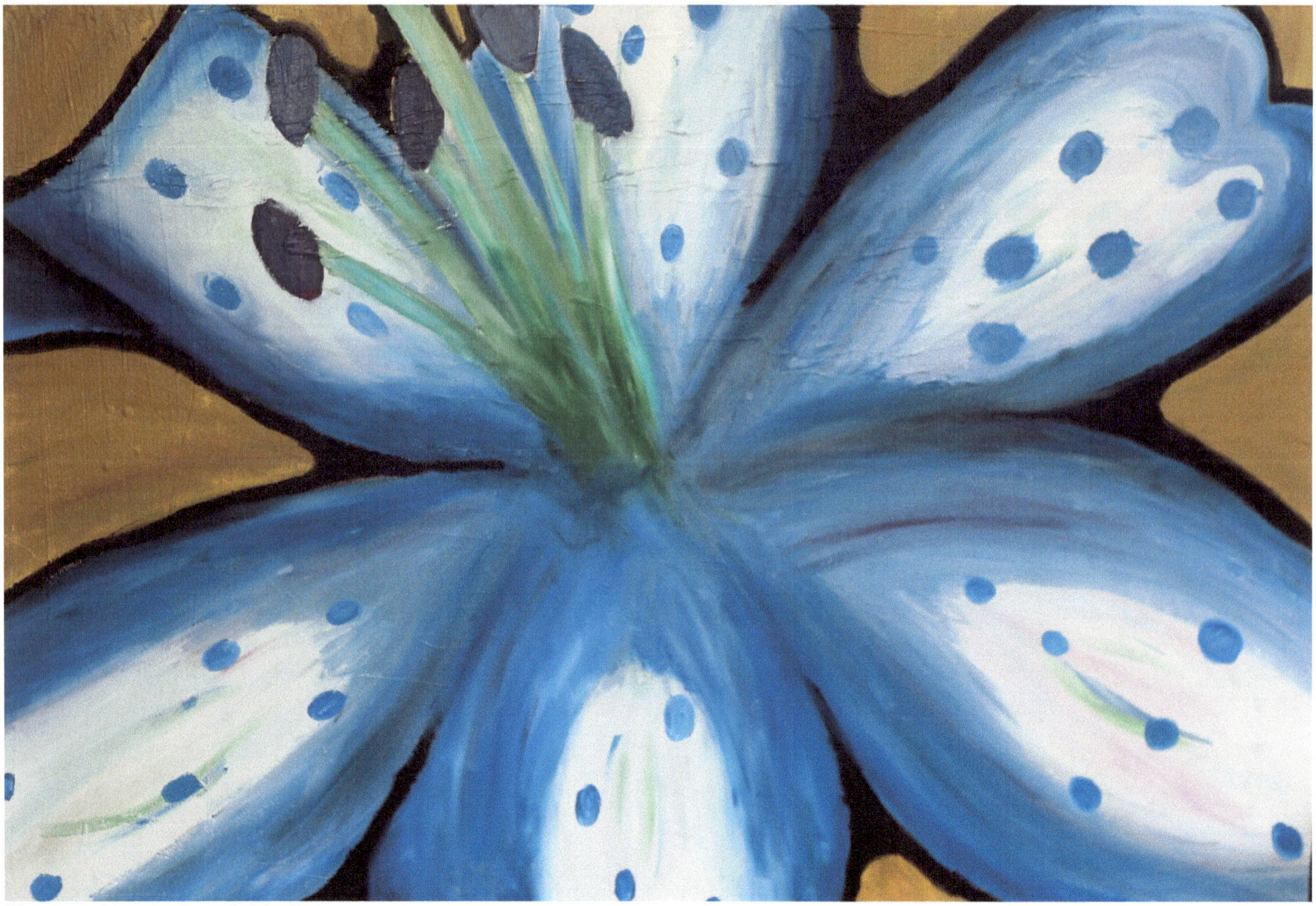

Illustrated by Audrey Fields, 7

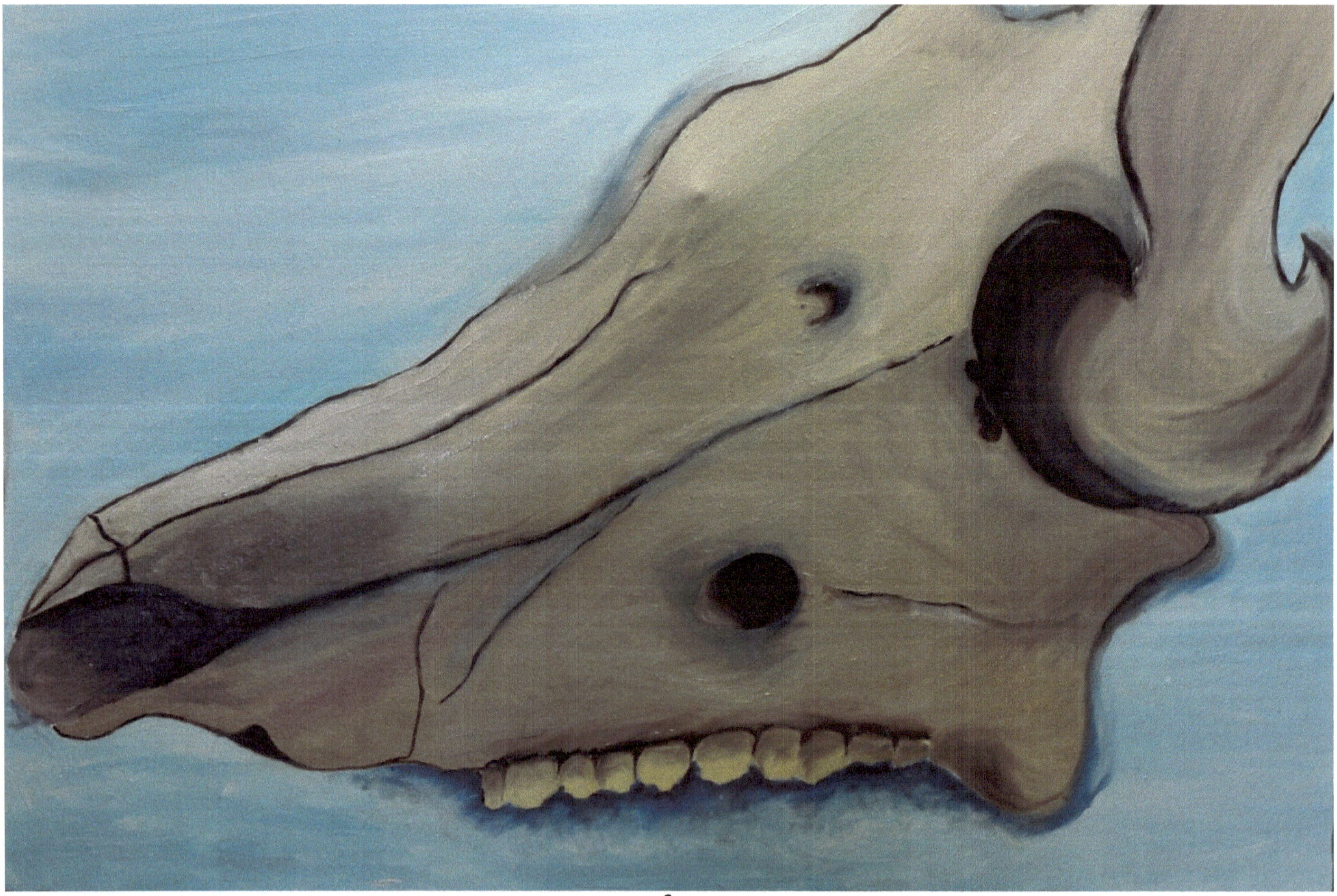

Illustrated by Ruby Wiggs, 8

Waking Dream

by **Kelly Waterbury-Gunn**, teacher

I am dreaming this haunting dream. It is the middle of the night, 2:30 am, maybe 3:00 A.M. and I wake from a deep sleep. It is early July, in a house with no air conditioning, so the windows are open wide to let in the cool night breeze. The house belongs to dear friends, but I've spent so much time here, it feels like home, and the rooms, the shadows, the smells are as familiar as those of my own home, back in Lexington.

I am standing beside the bed now, looking at my two youngest daughters, six-year-old twins who sleep soundly on either side, their bodies half wrapped in crumpled sheet, half uncovered and stretched comfortably, one arm thrown across a pillow, another tucked under the head. As I stand looking, I smell the faint smoke of what I perceive to be a distant trash heap burning in the neighbors' backyard. Not unusual for the country to have farmers burn their trash out back. I noticed in the same moment that I need to go the bathroom, so I turn from the bed, but instead of using the bathroom that is adjacent to the bedroom where I am sleeping, I choose to go out into the upstairs hallway.

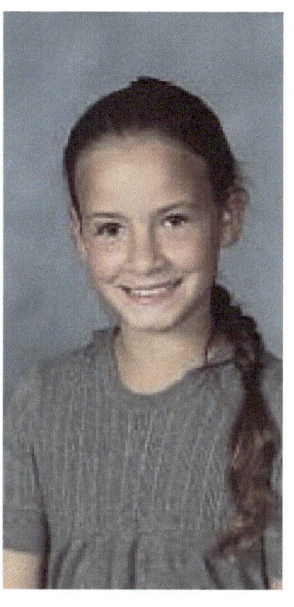

Audrey Fields, 7
Art Major

Grey, the family dog who had been sleeping on the tile floor of the upstairs bathroom, isn't there. My mind begins shuffling information. As I wash my hands at the white pedestal sink, I hear Sadie, the other family dog, barking from her kennel down in the living room. This is a 100-year-old Victorian home, so the sound is distant, but demanding of my attention. Now I'm awake in my dream, I am moving to the top of the main staircase, trying to discern why Sadie is barking and where Grey might be.

My two older daughters are sleeping in a room at the opposite end of the hall, some 50 feet across the upstairs landing. No one stirs. As I walk to the back hallway, the one that leads down the back staircase to the kitchen below, I hear something new. Something that changes my feeling from bothered to fearful. A sound like splitting wood, like an ax splintering a dry piece of wood, seems to be coming from the depths of the staircase. My

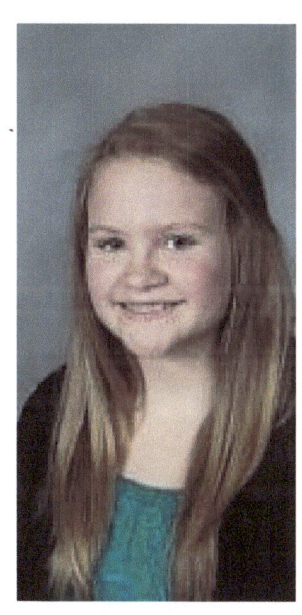

Ruby Wiggs, 8
Art Major

imagination seizes on this and considers how to respond if indeed someone is trying to break into the house. The dog barks incessantly.

I run tiptoe back to the bedroom and grab my track phone from the nightstand beside the bed. The twins haven't moved. I notice that I have only nine minutes left on the phone, so whatever I do, whoever I call, I better make it good. As I return to the top of the backstairs, I listen for the sound again. This time I realize it is not coming from below, but rather, from above. This shifts the thoughts in my head, and the idea of an intruder disappears, but now I am trying to imagine what could be in the attic that could cause that kind of noise. I stand outside the attic door listening intently. A raccoon could have gotten in through the broken attic window, or maybe a squirrel. I am hesitant to open the door, for fear that something might get into the house, but curiosity overpowers my fear. I carefully peek through a tiny crack in the door as I open it a fraction of an inch.

All that I had thought of so far, does not begin to prepare me for what was delivered to my vision. At the very top of the stairs, lapping at the oxygen rich air, and dancing like shining yellow waves, are the quickly spreading waves of a fire. Fire! Fire! My head is spinning, thoughts rushing everywhere like the flames, what to do first. Must call 9ll! Wake the girls! Where are the dogs? Call 911! How is this happening? Legs running, arms moving, pushing bodies to waking, "Girls, the house is on fire!" I hear myself saying in a clear calm direct voice. "Get your sisters and get out NOW! "Tynan, get the dogs! Hold on to Grey and put them both in the van. Go to the van!" I am moving all around as I wrap the twins in blankets, trying to keep them from being terrified, but recognizing that they

have just been startled from a deep sleep by the most frightening of conditions. As their older sisters bustle them down the front stairs and out into the night, I dial 911 and suddenly realize I don't know the street address of the house. I know it is on McCracken Pike. I know the farm is called Dufont. I know the driveway like the back of my hand, but I can't conger the number.

In a moment of enlightenment, I think of all the mail piled on the kitchen table, addressed to the Platts. I run to the dining room and read the address off to the person on the other end. I am trying to talk clearly and precisely. I hear myself saying, "Please hurry, hurry!" and I am moving, moving all around the house making sure the girls, the dogs, every living thing is out.

I am thinking of my friends. I am trying to think, how can I get things out? What would I take? What about all the furniture, the pictures, all the wonderful books, the picture of Flora in her wedding gown? Surely the firefighters will get here in time. Surely it hasn't gotten too big yet. Where did it start? What should I do? I try calling my husband, but he doesn't answer. I leave many messages, but never hear a voice. I call Jen, a mutual friend of the Platts and of us. I don't know where to go. I have four children and two terrified dogs in my van. We are half dressed. I run back upstairs and grab a bag with some clothes in it so the girls will be covered. Now I smell more smoke. SMOKE! That was what I had smelled. Now everything is coming together and I am falling apart. I grab my purse and my keys from the kitchen counter and run out the front door. I drive the van away from the house and pull over onto the grass so that we are facing the house from a distance.

That is when the attic windows explode. Flames are grabbing and hurling themselves out into the darkness, and I am listening for sirens. I am praying in my dream, "Oh, please God, please let them get here. Oh, please God, let them save the house. Please come, now, please!"

It is a long three minutes, and finally a lone police car comes driving up the driveway. I am panicking now. I roll down my window as he pulls up beside my van. He is asking me if everyone is out and I say yes. He is asking me my name, and I explain who I am and why I am there. He is asking so many questions and I am watching the house burning and, where is that fire truck? And why is this taking so long?

Two minutes later I hear the first siren and see the lights turning from the main road onto the driveway. They are moving fast and I see several firefighters jump off the truck and run around to the back of the house. They try to get up the stairs but it is already spreading down to the second floor. Seven minutes from the time I first called, part of the attic has fallen down into the second floor. I am telling the firefighters, there is a pond at the back of the farm and there is water in the swimming pool. I am fully aware that we are far from a real water source and it has been a very dry summer.

I look behind me in the van and four pairs of eyes are wide with fear and full of tears. They are all talking and crying at once, "But Mommy, what about the pictures? Mommy, what about all their things? What are they going to do? Mommy, what about our clothes! I left the computer in there, Mom! What about the cats?" Aedon screams as the second floor window in what was Sanders' bedroom, explodes, followed by another. Flames are everywhere and I tell the police officer we have to get out of here. The girls are terrified, the dogs are climbing all over us and I have to get to a place where we can calm down. We go to Jen's house, and I have no idea how I get to her house, because I am driving but I am not awake. I must be dreaming. This must be a dream. I will wake up. Please let me wake up!

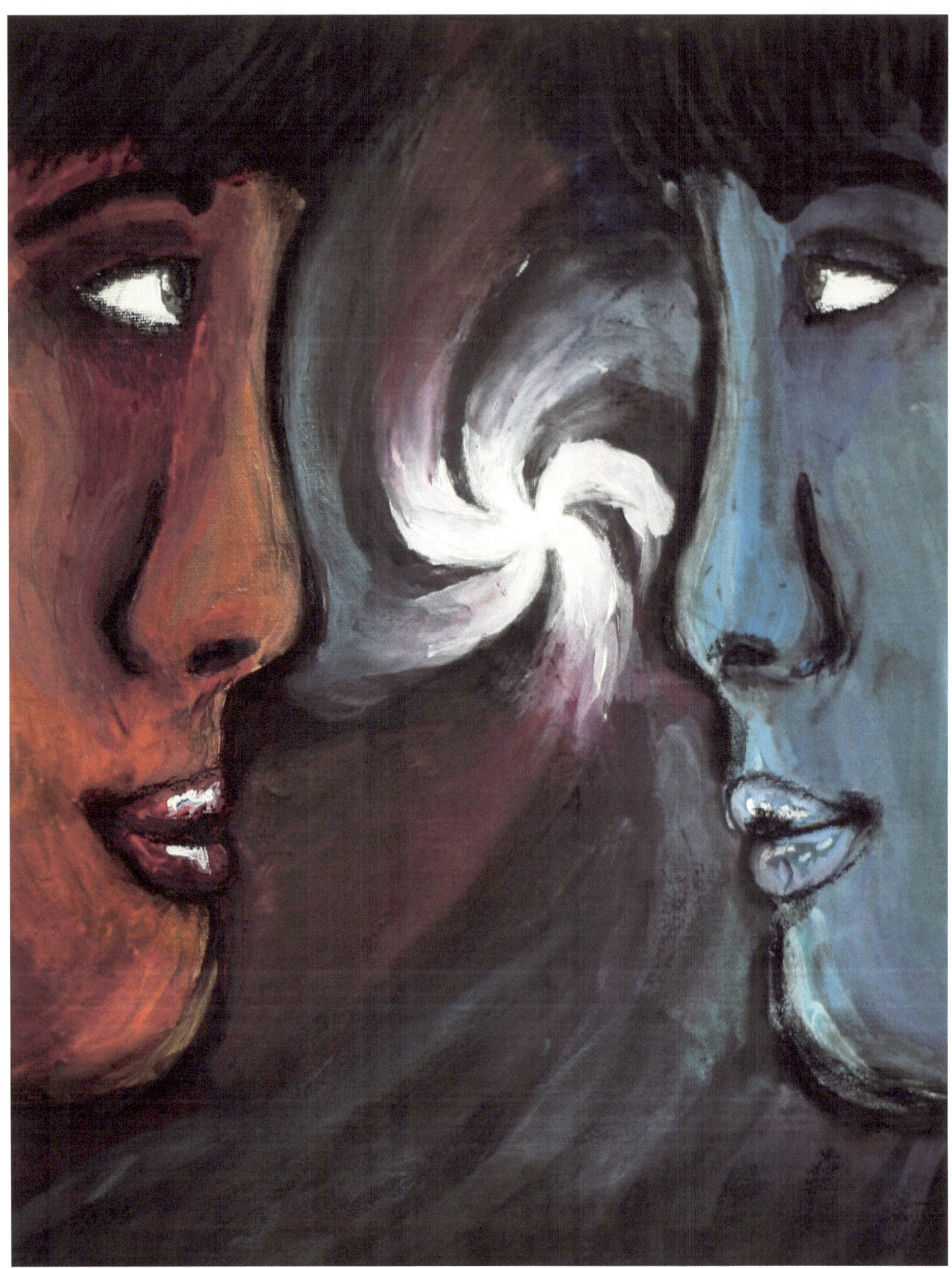

Illustrated by John Clark Baker, 7

Being 13-years-old

by Jahnavi Stivers, 8

Excited to be one-year older,

Tired to act more mature,

Lucky to be 13.

Frustrated about doing more chores,

Confused to be a teenager,

Glad to *finally* have more freedom.

Bored of being in middle school,

Sick of all the tests,

Disappointed with grades.

Sad to be 14 in one more day,

Surprised at the gained maturity,

Happy to have made it through your first teen year.

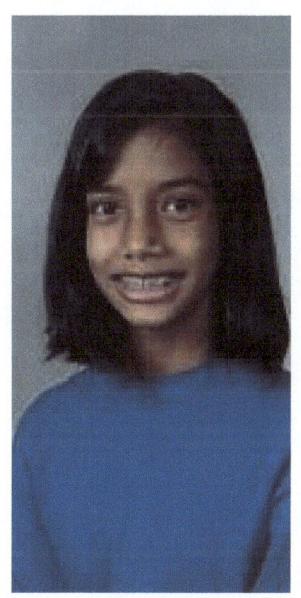

Jahnavi Stivers, 8
Creative Writing Major

My Bed

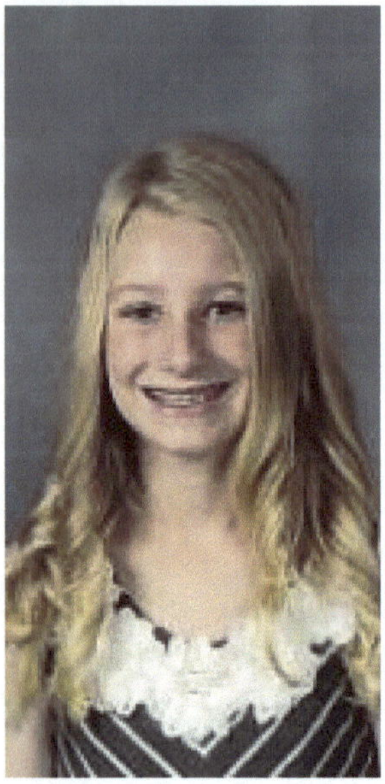

by Fiona Farrer, 6

A bouncy mattress,

Is all I need when my energy bursts into pieces.

A smooth sheet,

Is all I need to suck up all my sadness and anger.

A cozy comforter,

Is all I need to trap my feelings within.

A wool blanket,

Is all I need on a cold and blurry winter day.

A comfortable pillow,

Is all I need after a long and tiresome day.

My bed,

A home for my heart and soul.

Fiona Farrer, 6
Band Major

Memories

by Emma Cline, 5

What does it mean to have a memory?

Does it mean to remember a cherished moment?

Or to have a terrible reminder of something you've done?

No.

A memory is to remember the birth of a beloved moment,

Or a shadow of the regret and dark paths that were taken.

So, is a memory a blessing or a curse?

That's for you to decide.

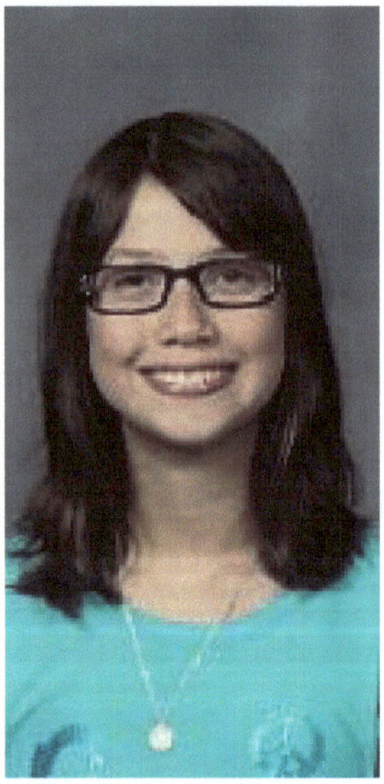

Emma Cline, 5
Creative Writing Major

Winter

by Taleah Gipson

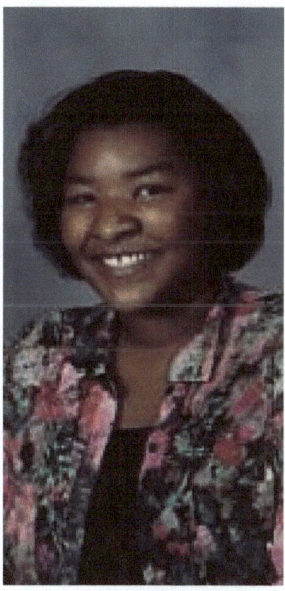

Taleah Gipson, 8
Creative Writing Major

Winter breeze.

Snow flakes

Instead of leaves.

The days are longer

So, the sun

can breathe.

Snowman,

Reindeer,

Santa clause,

Baking pies,

No more lies.

Coldness everywhere.

Hands in my pockets,

As I look around

exploring

the cold

Wonderland.

Book Review

by Amelia Loeffler, 6

Birdsall, Jeanne. *The Penderwicks: A Summer Tale of Four Sisters, Two Rabbits, and a Very Interesting Boy*. New York: Knopf, 2005. Print.

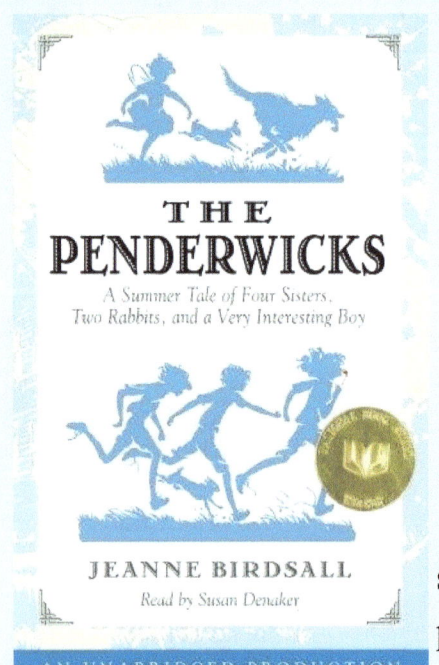

Amelia Loeffler, 6
Creative Writing Major

The Penderwicks: A Summer Tale of Four Sisters, Two Rabbits, and a Very Interesting Boy, tells the story of The Penderwick family summer vacation. The four sisters: Rosalind, Jane, Skye, Batty, and their father, Martin, hope to spend a somewhat relaxing three week vacation at the cottage they rent from the snooty owner of Arundel Estate. However, their stay is anything but relaxing. The sisters (and an unexpected friend) have an unforgettable summer, that is both adventurous and timeless. The sisters are unique in their own ways and will endear themselves to readers.

Jeffrey Tifton's mother owns the prestigious estate, and he easily becomes a close friend of the four girls with his likeable and humorous personality. Mrs. Tifton, on the other hand, retains a strict manner, determined to ensure that her son and his new acquaintances won't get into any trouble. If she thinks that the Penderwicks won't cause chaos during their summer vacation, then she has a lot to learn.

Jean Birdsall's novel perfectly captures the playful and energetic spirits of today's youth and creates a personal connection between the reader and the characters.

The Penderwicks won the National Book Award for Young People's Literature, and is part of a five book series.

"I Buried Paul"

by Ella Webster, 7

Birdsall, Jeanne. *The Penderwicks: A Summer Tale of Four Sisters, Two Rabbits, and a Very Interesting Boy*. New York: Knopf, 2005. Print.

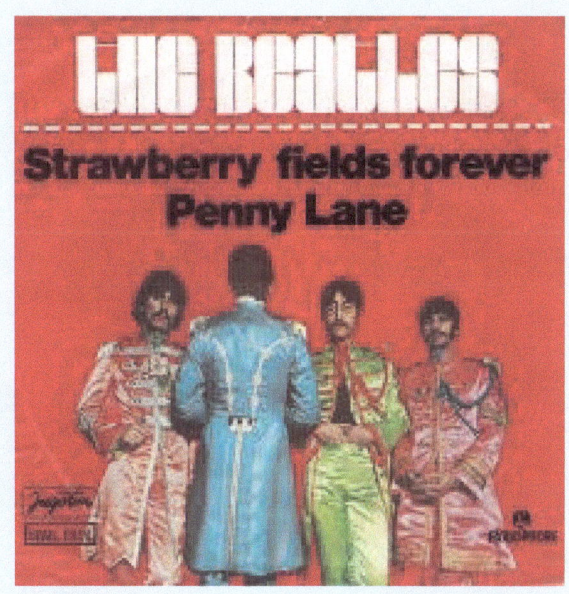

I n 1969, a rumor about the Beatles bass guitar player, Paul McCartney struck the world. It said that Paul McCartney was driving somewhere close to London and his car crashed. No one ever said how or why, but apparently it went up in flames and took McCartney's life. Nowadays, people have different opinions on the rumor, but there happen to be some supporting "evidence" that the believers have found in the album covers and in the songs.

It seems to be that on every album made after Paul's rumored death, there is at least one clue as to whether or not he could have died. One of the albums that had the most 'clues' is The Beatle's *Abbey Road* album that debuted just after his "death". The cover art with all of the Beatles walking in a line had many supporting suspicions. One is that Paul McCartney is walking out of step with the others, is the only one barefoot, and is holding a cigarette. The only reason why the cigarette is supporting evidence because he was holding it in his *right* hand, when he really is *left* handed.

Another album with many clues to Paul's death was the album *Sgt. Peppers Lonely Hearts Club Band.* In the cover picture, someone's hand is over McCartney's head. This is said to be a sign that he is being 'blessed' like at a real funeral. Another supposed clue is that the flowers on the ground is in the shape of a guitar- a left handed bass guitar. Paul played one just like this, and the Guitar has three strings instead of four. Four strings mean *all* the members of the band, but Paul has no string. An alternative unusual thing about the cover is that Paul is the only Beatle that isn't at an angle with the camera, and it looks as if he is being propped up.

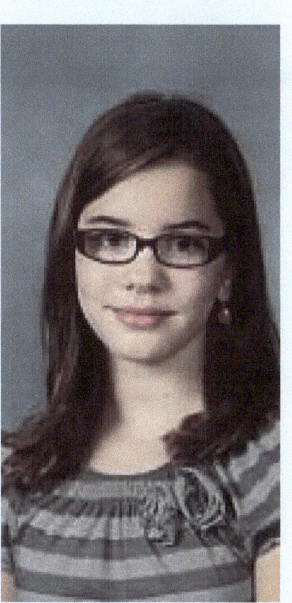

Ella Webster, 7
Strings Major

Later, another clue was "found" in the song *Strawberry Fields*. In the end, John Lennon mumbles something. When played slowly, it sounds as if he was saying "I buried Paul". Ironically, the believers were wrong and Lennon really said, "Cranberry Sauce"!

These so called clues are all very mysterious and easy to have confidence in. However, in late 1969 Paul spoke out, "I am alive and well" he explained. Some found this hard to believe. Many were convinced at this point that his death did not happen and they gave into his speech as proof. As I stated, there were different opinions. But is Paul McCartney alive today? Yes, yes he is. And fortunately, and he is still a great, left-handed, bass guitar player.

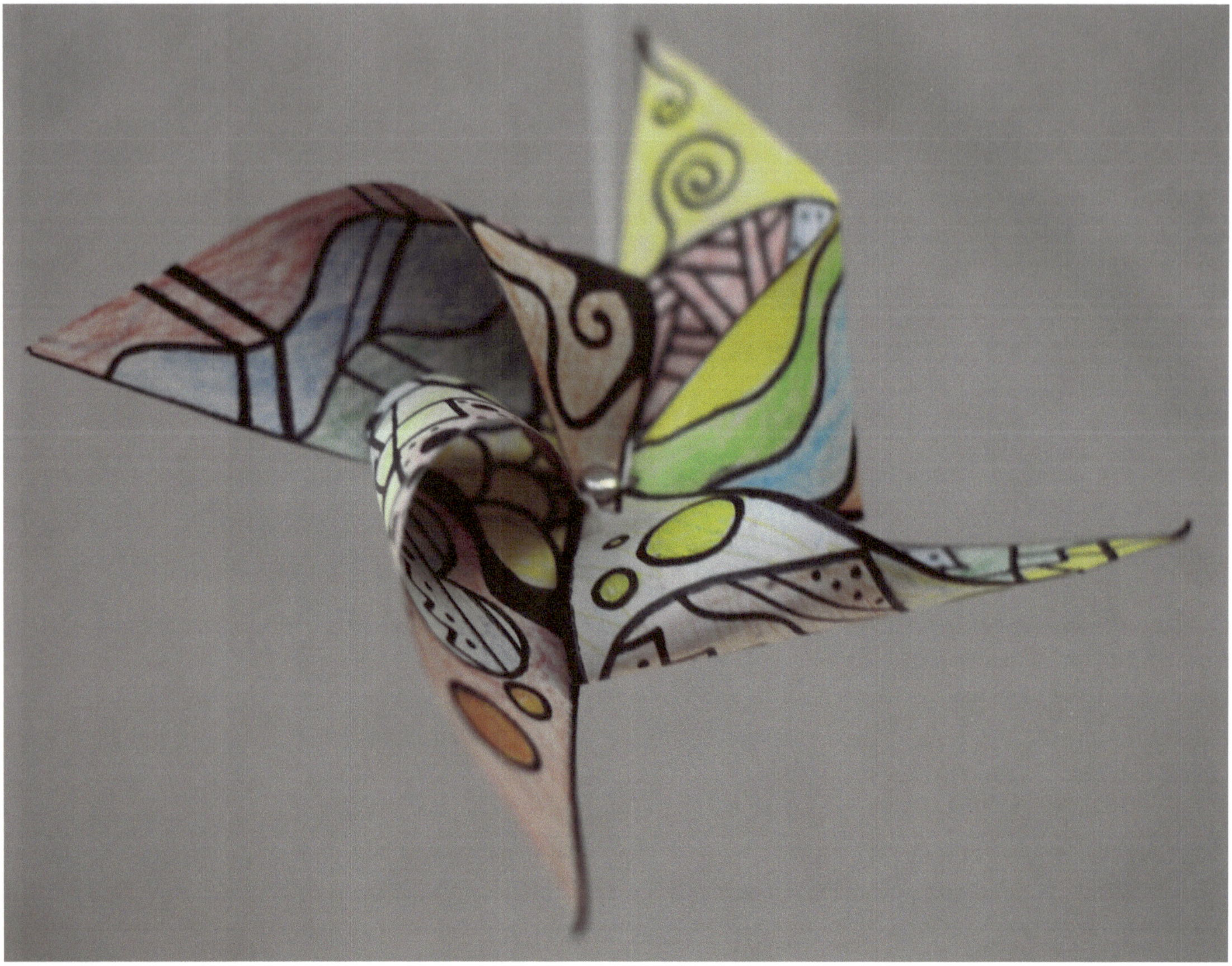

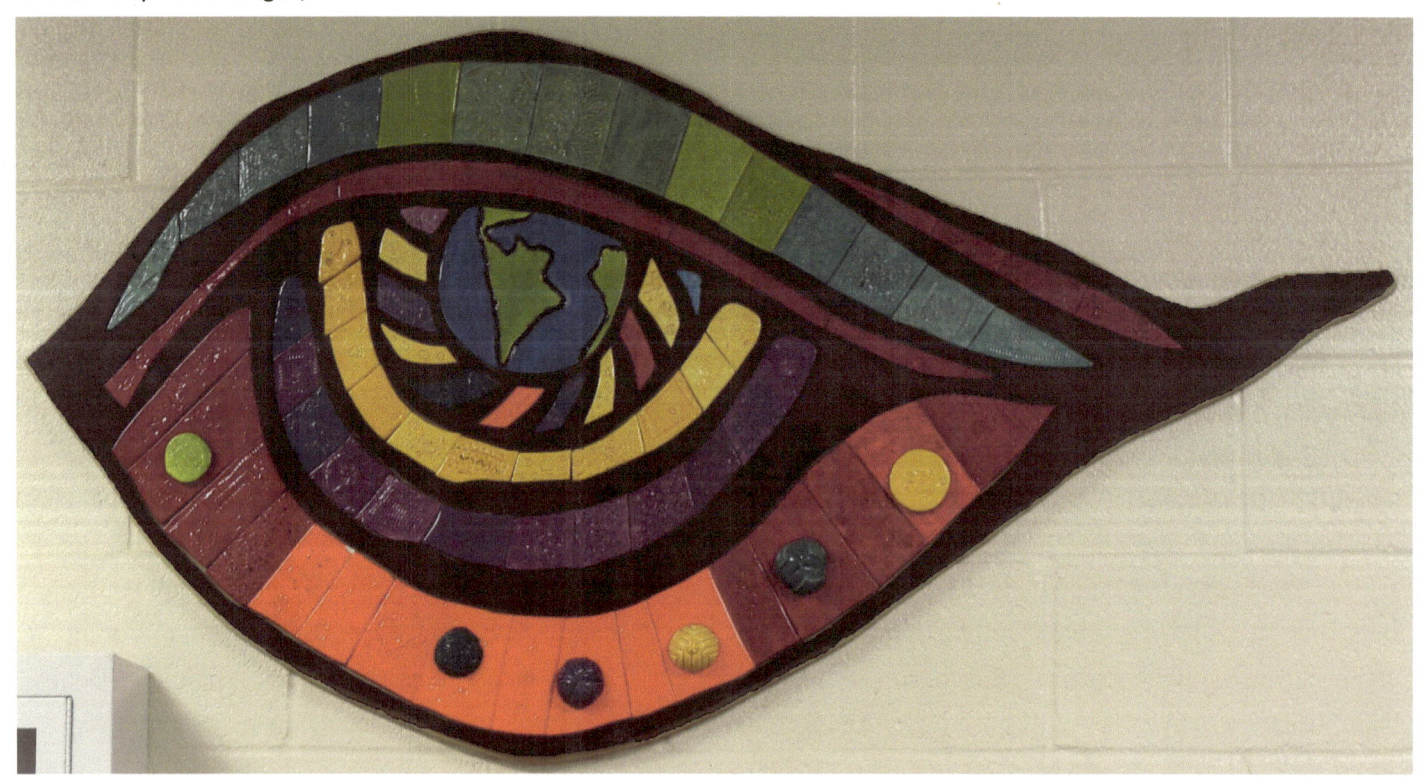

Illustrated by Anna Gilligan, 7

Illustrated by Mrs. Sosby's class

Letter to Beth Randolph

by Jacob Chapman, 7

Dear Ms. Randolph:

As a scholar at SCAPA Bluegrass, I have had experience that getting to our classes can sometimes be a hassle. The same could go for morning classes. In this letter, I will explain my schedule and how the timeframe can be stressful on students and how I wish we students had a longer amount of time to get to our classes.

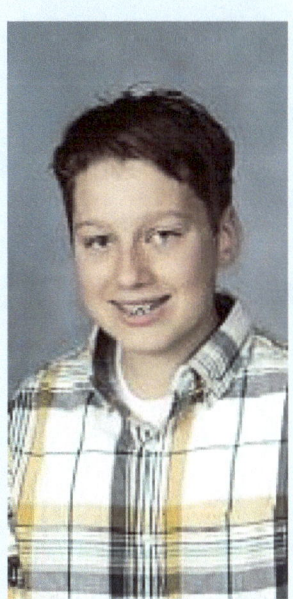

Jacob Chapman, 7
Creative Writing Major

As a Spanish student with Mrs. Karen Joly, I go to my classes after 3rd and 6th period. After my rotation class (3rd period), I head to my locker to pick up my lunch. In my opinion, that time is not stressful because we are only heading to lunch, where we get a tranquil break to talk and joke with are our peers. But after 6th period, the foreign language class, I am hastily shoving things into my bag; hoping it's what I need for homework. Then I race down to the Creative Writing room before the tardy bell rings so I'm not scolded for being late.

When I get home and go through my backpack and realize that I forgot my Social Studies textbook or my unit folder for Science, which is required for other homework I begin to stress. Stress is tension felt by somebody, it could be mental, emotional, or physical. For me, I can't sleep, and I have to worry about it the next morning or add it to tomorrow's homework. Point is, forgetting things in your locker you'll need for homework just isn't enjoyable.

But, this is only for Spanish students. I cannot speak for the French students, but Kayla Buchignani will happily apply. Kayla says that she has trouble getting to her classes sometimes and getting all of her stuff for French. She has to grab all of her stuff and pack her backpack and, like me, can't get to her class on time.

My solution to this problem is creating a five minute break time to go to our lockers or next class. I believe this idea will work because "A minute may not seem like a lot, but a minute is a lot" –Anonymous. Giving middle school students this extra minute will decrease tardiness and upset students. Having four minutes may seem like quite a long time to go to your locker, if you're on the same floor as your class! If you have to go all the way upstairs to grab something, that would be quite a hassle. I believe some students have to do this, and I don't think they enjoy it.

Now most students are getting into the flow of school, but some haven't mastered the technique of their locks. For some students, unlocking their lockers is like breathing. But for the ones who still have trouble, they have to really rush because it has already taken those two minutes to unlock their locker and now they have to pack up their stuff to get to their next class. Celina Luo says she kept turning her locker's lock backward, taking her ten to fifteen minutes or so to get it open by herself. Eventually, she had to ask a peer or teacher to help. Celina says she wasn't scolded by her teachers because it was the first day of school, but you can imagine how a younger student having trouble getting their locker open would feel.

So giving the five minute break for students to go to their lockers would also improve student's moods too. Not having to worry about being late or getting in trouble would boost their self-esteem, also helping them concentrate better in their classes. This is why I think the five minute break should become a new system for SCAPA Bluegrass; it is the ideal solution through my eyes.

Yours truly,

Jacob A. Chapman

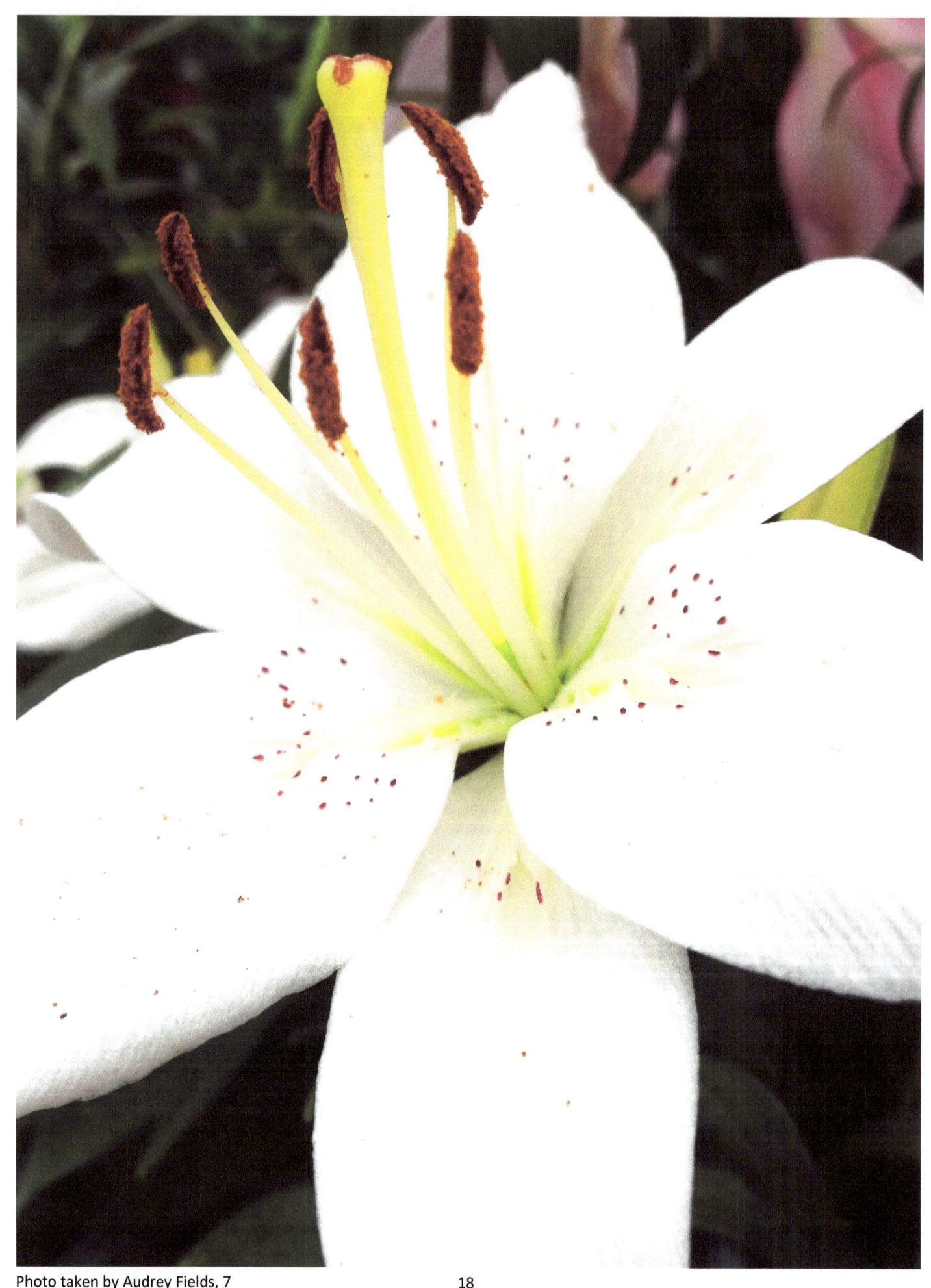

Photo taken by Audrey Fields, 7

My Summer Vacation

by Taylor Trapp, 7

It was in the middle of the day and Allie was at the pool…

My friend Allie and I went on summer vacation together to Lake Barkley, and we were staying in the queen suite, a cabin over the water that my grandma received for being Lexington's region four vice president in the council she is involved in.

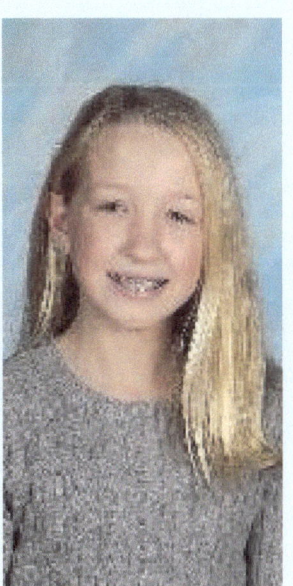

Taylor Trapp, 7
Creative Writing Major

There is a talent show every year, and Allie and I were practicing to perform our gymnastics. The previous year, my friend Christina and I made up a mime act for the talent show, but ended up not doing it. So this year I saw Christina and went to say hi, while all this time Allie was at the pool. I invited Christina into our room because it was the nice thing to do. We started to practice our old mime act and ended up in a pillow fight somehow.

She knocked my pillow out of my hands, and when it rolled under the table I went to pick it up. I bent under the table and started to stand up, but Christina hit my lower back and I went jeering into the table. It hurt, so I put my hand over my eye and my face into the pillow, but I didn't cry.

Finally, my friends noticed that I was in pain. Christina rushed to me and pleaded, "Let me see it! Let me look at it."

She reached for my hand and pulled my face up. She immediately started watching my eye drip with blood and saw my hand with a pool of blood in it.

"Oh… your eye is bleeding!" She sounded scared.

I ran to the bathroom to see how deep it was and to put pressure on it.

"Go get, Allie!" I informed her with authority. She nodded and ran off. I looked at the blood soaked tissue and reached for another to put over my wound.

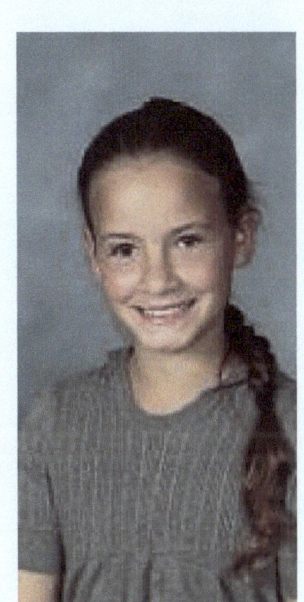

Audrey Fields, 7
Art Major

"Let me see how deep it is," Allie asked after running to my side.

I hesitated to show her but removed the tissue slowly.

She released a breath slowly and she said calmly, "You're OK. It's not that deep."

"My grandparents are in a meeting either in the Conference building or the main building," I replied, thankful that my scrape was not as deep as I thought.

My friends told me later that they had run down to the conference building and my grandparents weren't there; that took five to ten minutes. Then they ran to the main building and up the three flights of stairs and asked the administrator if

Charlie and Becky Murphy (my grandparents) were there.

"Why, is it really important?" the woman had asked, eying them.

"Yes! Taylor, their granddaughter, hit her head and is bleeding!" Allie spoke up.

The lady ran into the meeting and yelled for everyone to hear. "Taylor cracked her head open at the pool!"

My grandparents jumped up as fast as they could and ran down the stairs, because if you hear that your child cracks their head open you get this scary image. While I was in the room, I started feeling kind of dizzy and decided to sit down. Then I realized I wanted some fresh air, so I opened the front door and saw all four of them running down the steps and into the room.

They came into the living room while Christina explained what happened. Papaw, my grandfather, was so worried he almost sounded mad. Allie ran down the hall to get ice to help the swelling. Yep that's right; I was going to have a big fat black eye!

Later that night Allie went down to the pool and I lay in bed watching T.V. Afterword, I got up and asked my grandpa, "Can we go down to Mrs. Ann's room and get some brownies?" Mrs. Ann was one of my grandparent's coworkers.

"Sure," he said with a smile. We got up and went to Mrs. Ann's room and got chess bars and brownie bars. Even though I almost had to go to the emergency room, I had a great summer vacation, and Allie and I even ended up getting second place in the competition. Despite the injury I obtained during vacation, my summer was great.

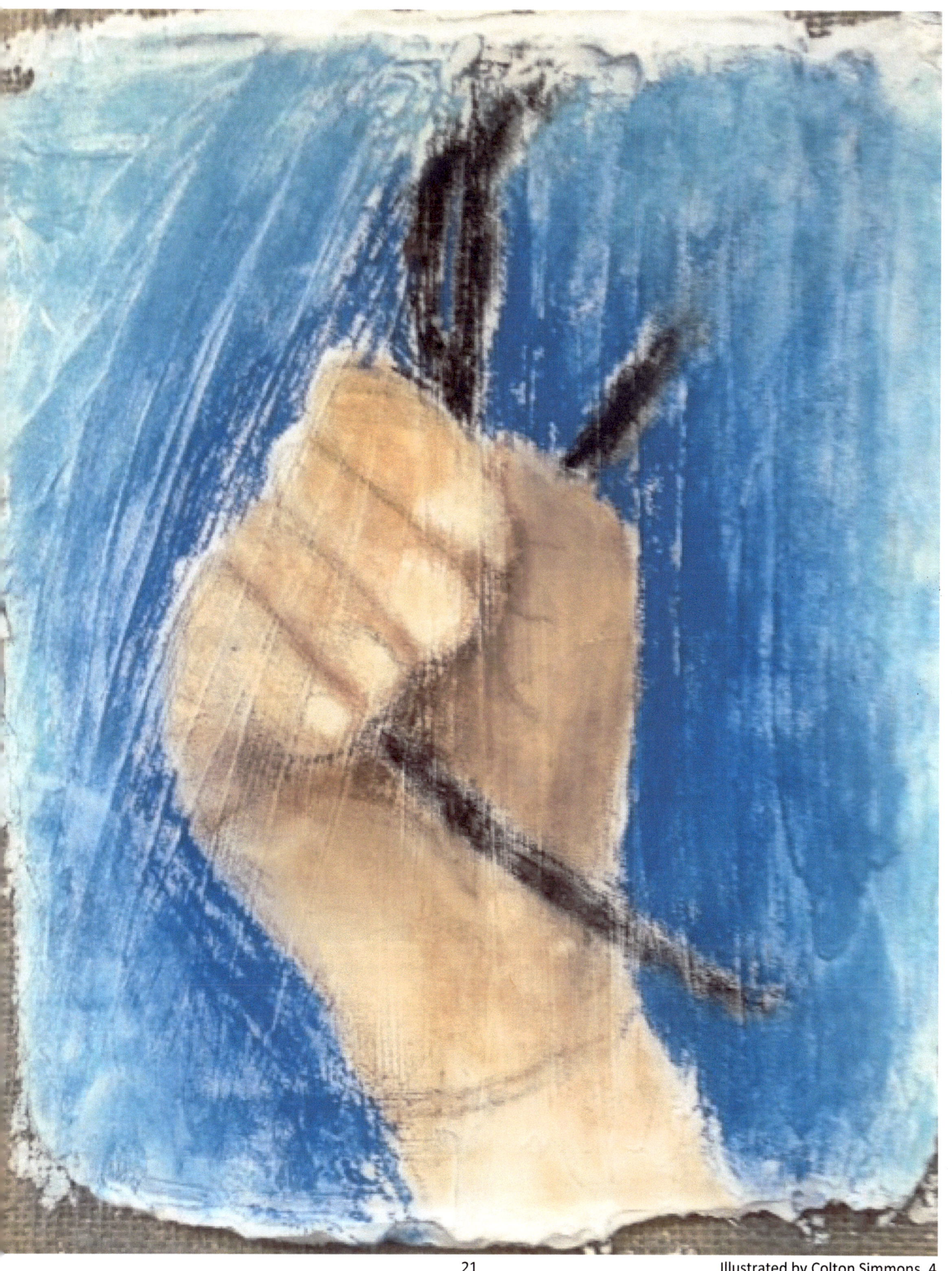

Illustrated by Colton Simmons, 4

Ruach: Spirit, Wind, Breath

by Andrea Stang, teacher

Slowing down, I let my concentration fall back to my body, the rhythm of my steps and cadence of my breaths. I felt faint. My head spun, but I focused on the sound of my soles landing on the pavement. Groaning, I forced my feet to stay in motion and my lungs to maintain their constant influx of air.

Breath. That was life. But at the time I considered running to be my life. A teenager sees her hobbies as what defines her. She doesn't look much further than that, dig much deeper. I didn't realize that my definition would switch to the next slide so quickly. The transition was not smooth like a digital slideshow. It was more like an old Kodak Carousel, swiftly, but noisily lugging the new image into place, gears resisting throughout the process.

When the cancer came, it swept away my identity. A hurricane clearing away the coast. Sickness wasn't supposed to happen to young people, to healthy people, to strong and kind people. It made me question everything I had thought I was. I had to force myself to breathe.

In the Torah, the word "Ruach" is translates into "spirit of God." But this word has other meanings: wind, mind, and breath. Each translator chooses a different meaning, which changes the interpretation of the text. The ruach is present in God's other major acts in Genesis, in which he creates light by uttering a word, a breath, or when he creates a human by breathing life into Adam.

Ruach is strength and temper and anger, coolness, courage, and heart. It is inspiration and motivation, trustworthiness, and wrath. We are exposed in our need for air. It happens both deliberately and involuntarily. It quickens with anxiety and slows with relaxation. Its intake illustrates surprise and fear. Its exhalation expresses exhaustion and discontent.

It is a wind blown forth from the soul, one that carries carbon dioxide. Air embraces us intimately. It joins all life together. We breathe the same argon atoms that Ghandi and Cleopatra and Shakespeare did.

It's no coincidence that a strong metaphor is "breathing life into" inanimate objects. Breath can also be "taken away" by awe and wonder-filling sights and experiences.

Air is only felt in motion and is itself tasteless.

Humans can survive a month without food, a week without water, but only a few minutes without air. We are tiny specks on stardust in the grand scheme and air is what keeps us alive. And yet we take it for granted. We hyperventilate when we're nervous. We sigh when we're annoyed. We heave great gulps of it when we're upset. How often do we breathe it in consciously and gratefully? How often did I? Seldom before my battle, and although I would like to say frequently now. It's just not true. As much as I try to remember to be deliberate in my breaths, life takes me away and it makes a habit out of breathing, and yet I am so thankful for that habit, for the easy way in which my chest rises and falls most often imperceptibly. But it's gratifyingly noticeable during momentous occasions of my life. Ruach flows within and around me. With and without me.

Breaking Free

by Sarah Yohe, 7

And in that moment, she broke free. All the stress, all the burdens, lifted off her shoulders by the hands of God. Big and curious, her eyes shone like two crystal rivers flowing through a diamond forest, and the sea of blue glittered in the tropical sun. Her dimples shyly appeared and her little nose wrinkled as it was tickled by the new grown grass. She let her hair down and it flared out- thick, long, and curly. Her legs were tangled within each other like two inseparable cords and her arms were outstretched as far as they could go. She laughed, and sighed a refreshing sigh of relief as she let go and became the giggly teenage girl she was destined to be. She didn't have a care about what was going on as she frolicked through the pasture and let the tall weeds tickle her shins. Her body relaxed, opening the opportunity for her to twirl, and dance, and roll around. Her true colors were pouring out of her like a tri-colored waterfall and her emotions seeped through her like orange juice emerging from the beaten skin of an overly gripped orange. Shouting, running, leaping for happiness she rose from the ashes and broke free. Broke free from the society she was bred into where perfection was plastered on every wall and negativity at every corner. Where the Easter Bunny and the Tooth Fairy didn't exist to the children anymore and all that did was IPhones and IPads and IPods. Where people couldn't read, where people couldn't write, where 90% of humans didn't like what their life turned out to be. For once, instead of letting the fear overcome her, she overcame the fear and tore away from that intruding society. That unlawful, rude, lying, despicable society. She broke free.

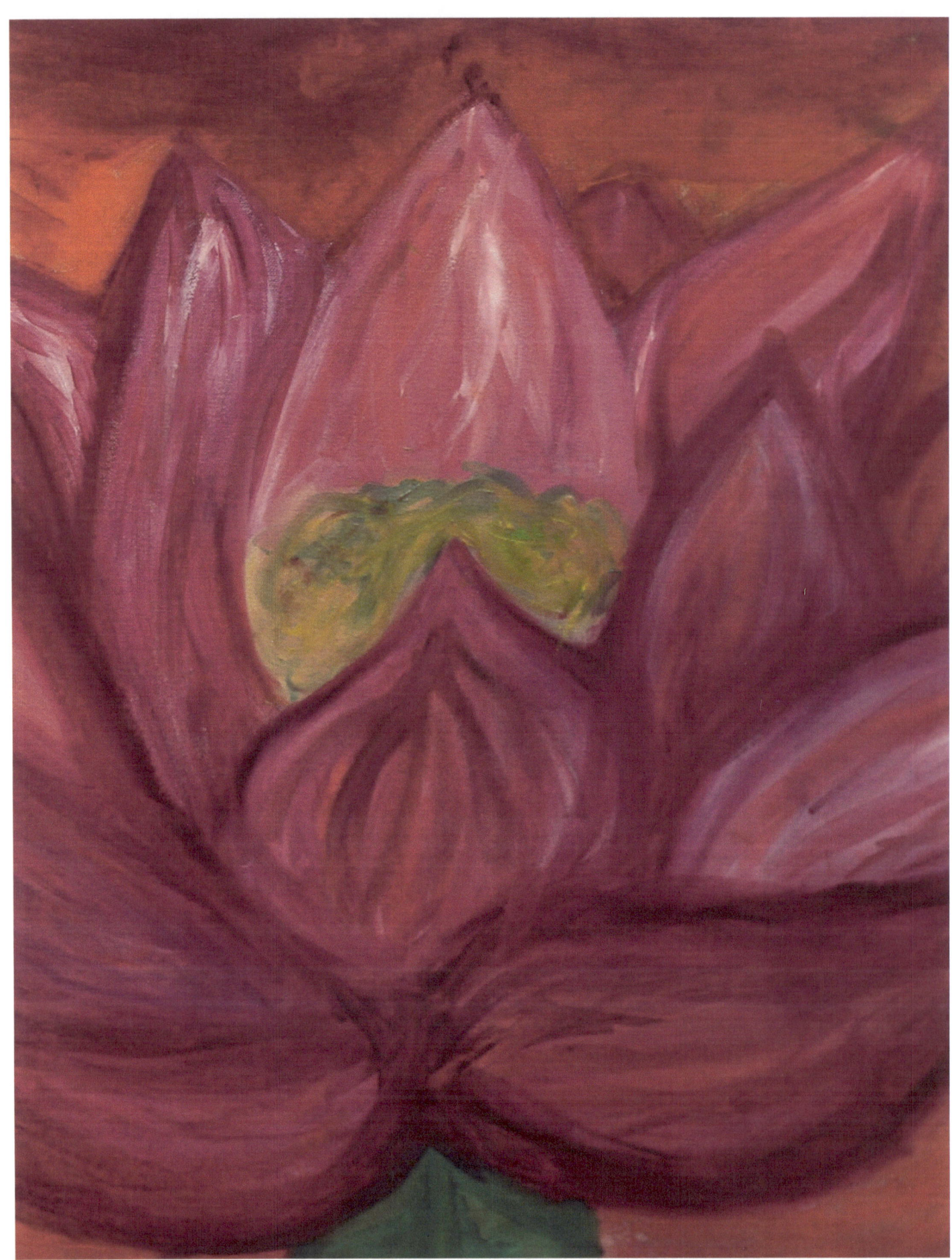

Illustrated by Andrew Gayheart, 6

Our World Today

by Katherine Cherry, 6

I would not want to live in a world with only joy and happiness,

Nor would I want to live in a world with only grief and despair.

When they meet in the middle they create harmony,

Where we learn every day from our similarities and our differences,

Which creates our world today.

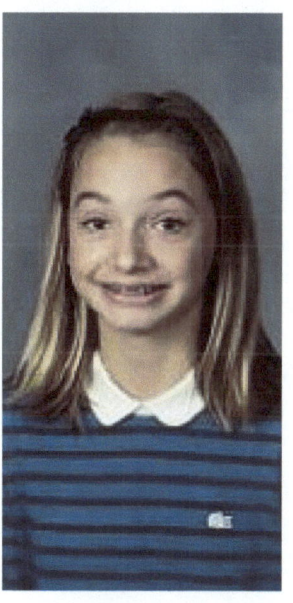

Katherine Cherry, 6
Strings Major

Be who your Heart Desires

by Gabby Prince, 4

Be

who your heart

Desires.

Not what everyone else

Is like.

You are your

Own person.

I guess what I'm

Saying is,

Be Yourself

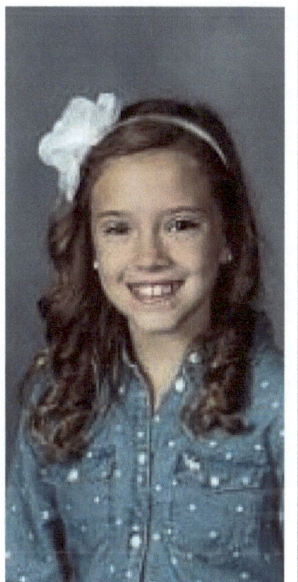

Gabby Prince, 4
Contemporary Dance Major

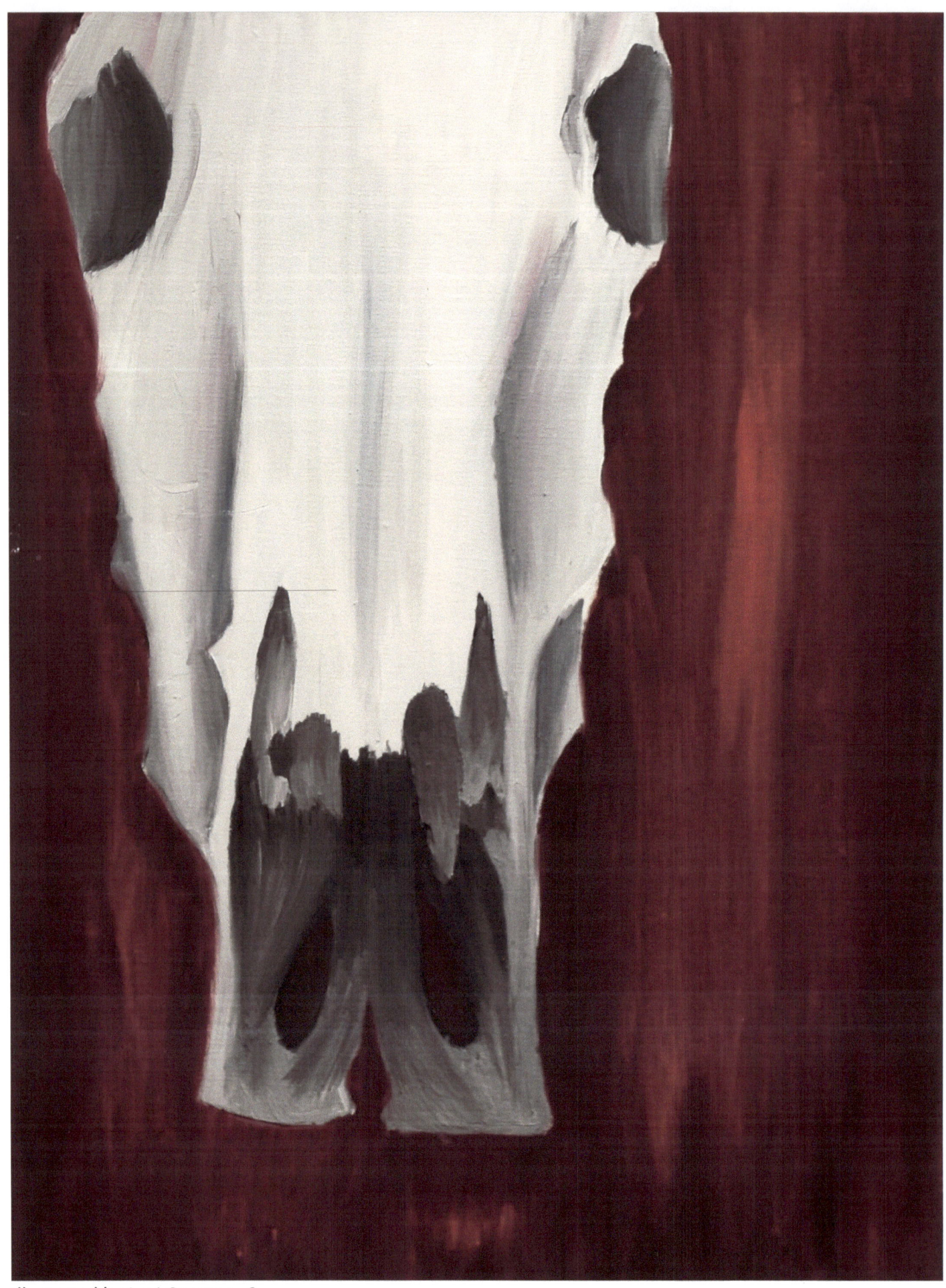

Illustrated by Lexi Ocampo, 6

What is Burning in Your Soul?

by Anonymous

We must now see this binding spell.

This curse.

This chain.

This poison.

We must

Think of it as a gift.

We must

Think of it as a light.

Now we accept it in its truest form.

Now that we know we can never go back.

It is no *poison.*

It is no *burden.*

It is no *problem.*

It is **fear**.

This is **love**.

In its truest form.

Our curse.

Our chain.

Our fatal flaw.

It is not love itself,

But it is **fear** of having none at all.

The Future

by Ruby Tevis, 8

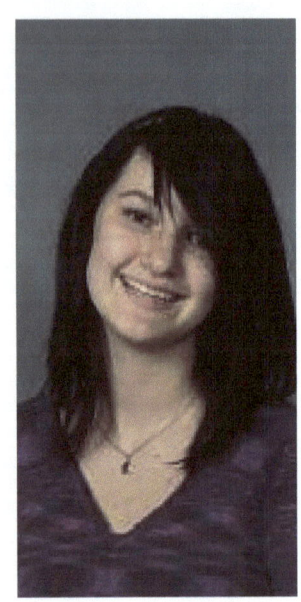

Ruby Tevis, 8
Creative Writing Major

The trees sway back and forth in the swirling wind,

That blows colored leaves in the direction of the west.

Curling over each other before they land perfectly sprawled

across one another.

Each leaf a day past.

The piled leaves create a red and orange fire,

Consuming the air like passing time.

The gray smoke burns the whites of your eyes as you gaze

into the horizon.

You stroll through the blooming meadow,

Towards the rising sun.

You walk into your future,

And forget the burning past that flares brighter with each

step you take.

Recipe for Friendship

by Deya Andreev and Riley Gossage, 4

Ingredients:

    1 cup common interests

    4 teaspoons loyalty

    3 tablespoons honesty

    1 BIG fight

    1 FAT resolution

    2 teaspoons secrets

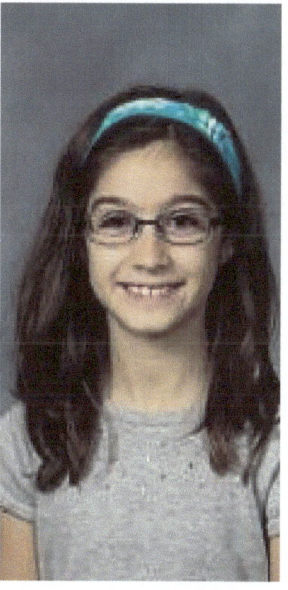

Deya Andreev, 4
Creative Writing Major

Directions:

First, mix together 1 cup common interests with 4 teaspoons loyalty, 3 tablespoons honesty, and 2 teaspoons secrets.

Then, when mixture gets thick, add 1 big fight. After that gets smooth, add 1 fat resolution.

Bake for 1 week or longer depending on person/personality

WARNING! Do not buy ingredients because "money don't buy you happiness"

" " = song

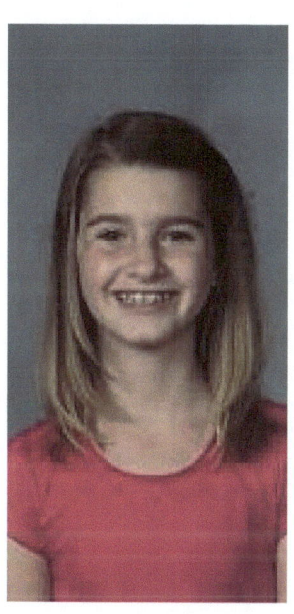

Riley Gossage, 4
Creative Writing Major

What Must He Think?

by Keith Lindsey, Teacher

Up under bullet-proof glass on a wall in the Louvre

is a work smaller than its reputation,

that depicts a smile the subject cannot contain.

And the genius responsible, master of shadow and line,

must wonder from his grave why Mona Lisa lives as she does,

removed from the world that she loved.

Up under magnets on the refrigerator door

is a drawing larger than life

that conveys the joie de vivre of a child not yet six.

And the genius responsible, having just mastered coloring inside the lines

must wonder from his grave why Mommy lives as she does,

removed from the world that he loved.

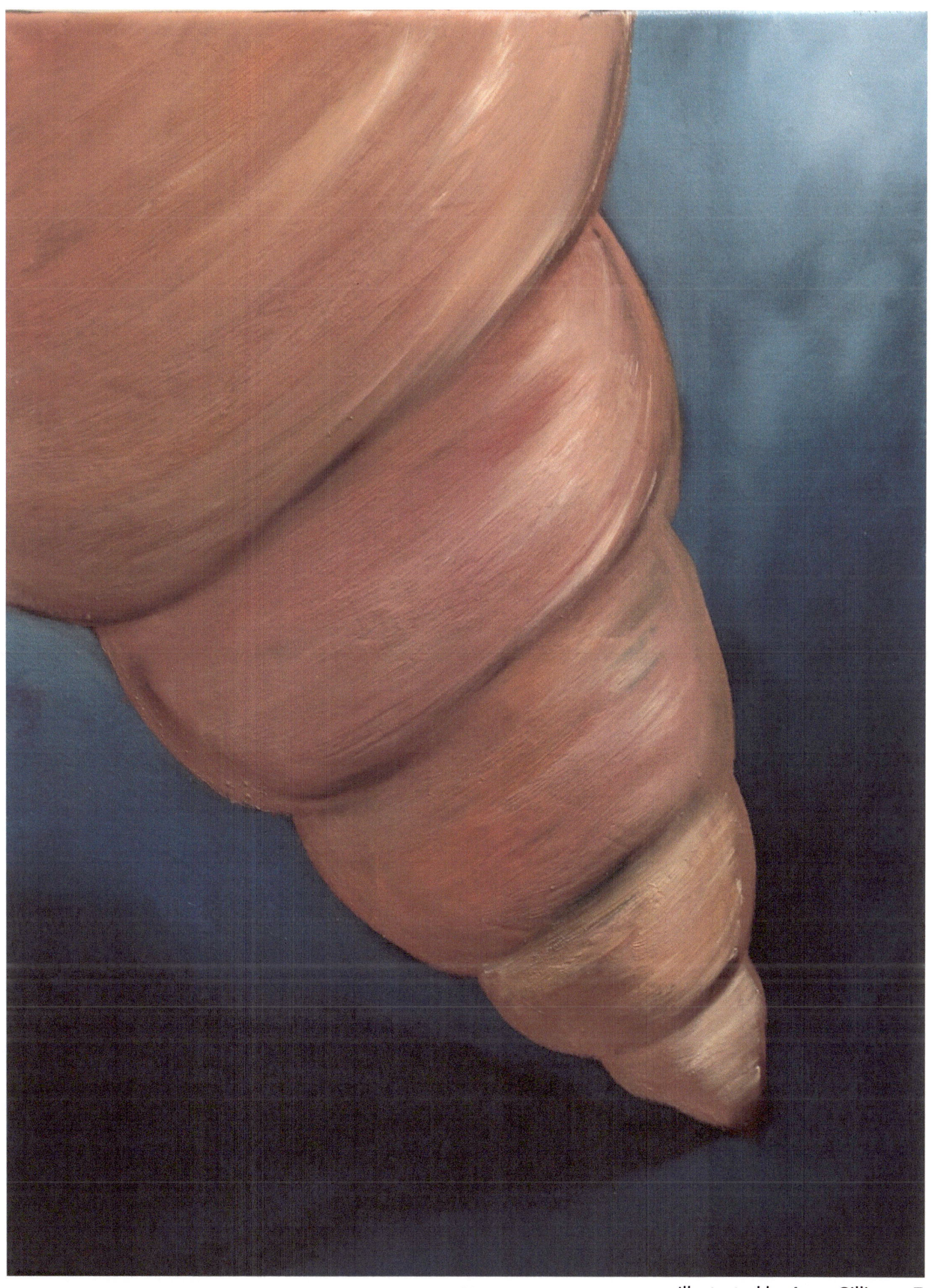

Illustrated by Anna Gilligan , 7

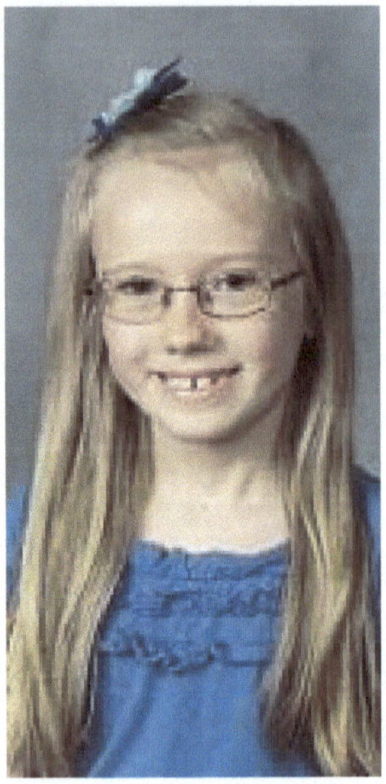

Autumn Leaves

by Elizabeth Weber, 4

Autumn leaves are falling,

Red, yellow, brown.

Autumn leaves are falling,

Swirling to the ground.

Autumn leaves are falling,

I gasp as they come down.

Autumn leaves are falling,

There is beauty all around.

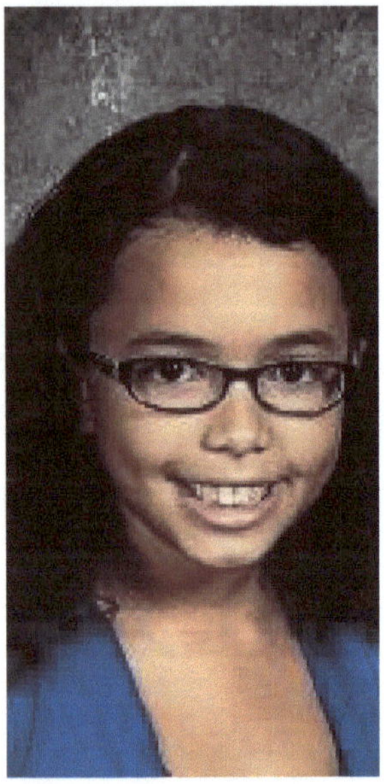

Elizabeth Weber, 4
Piano Major

Ballerinas

by Sophia Vaskuhl, 4

They whirl.

They twirl.

They leap.

And skip.

Oh! No! One's

About to trip.

I've never seen

Such a sight.

Those ballerinas

In the moonlight.

Sophia Vaskuhl, 4
Art Major

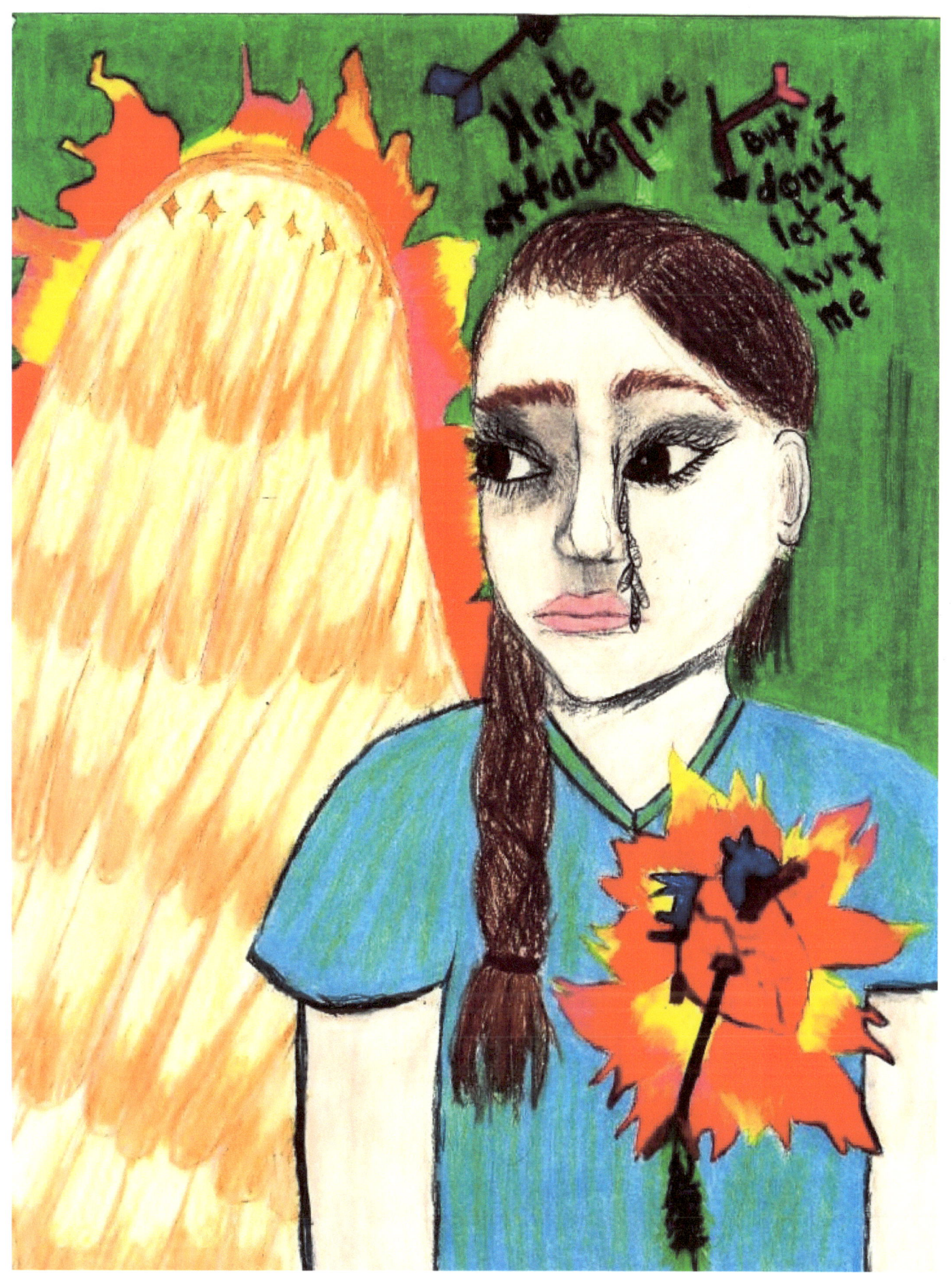

Illustrated by Nolan Gunn, 6

Seed

by Hali Horvath, 4

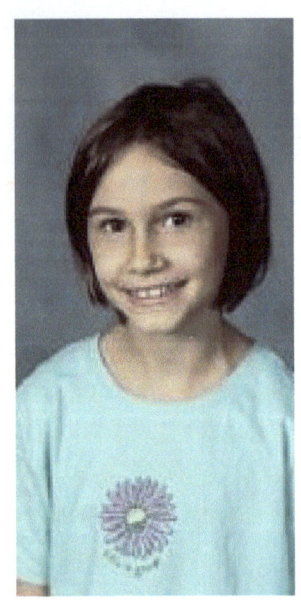

Hali Horvath, 4
Creative Writing Major

I am a seed,

Not a weed,

Or a plane,

Or the state of Maine,

I started on a journey,

About a mile ago,

Looking for a place to land,

Oh, where shall I go?

I don't want a place,

With now or sand,

I just want to find some,

Plain land,

How, now, where,

Where should I go?

I'll pay you a buck,

To drive me home.

Winter

by Fiona Daniel, 5

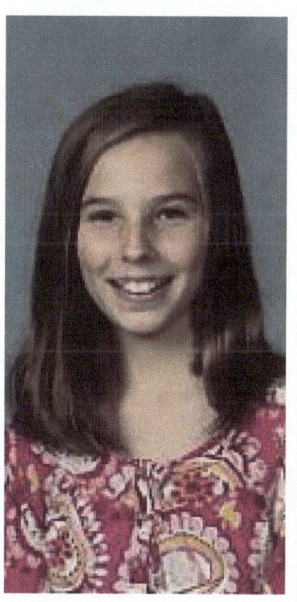

Fiona Daniel, 5
Creative Writing Major

As I sit on the side of the road, famished with hunger

As the winds whistle, carrying the aroma to the stomach

People walking on the side of the road like the winds drifting

through the clouds

As the words mean something to my heart, the friends I had

As my frizzy hair brushes to the left side, the opposite of my life

My tear hides from the light of the day

My heart starts to fade away of hope

The sun will not shine on me like there is shadow blocking my way

I start to lay lazily on the brick wall with no more energy

As I start to close my teary eyes slowly

My blood is going to stop slowly soon

As I look at the people slowly, but that was my last glimpse

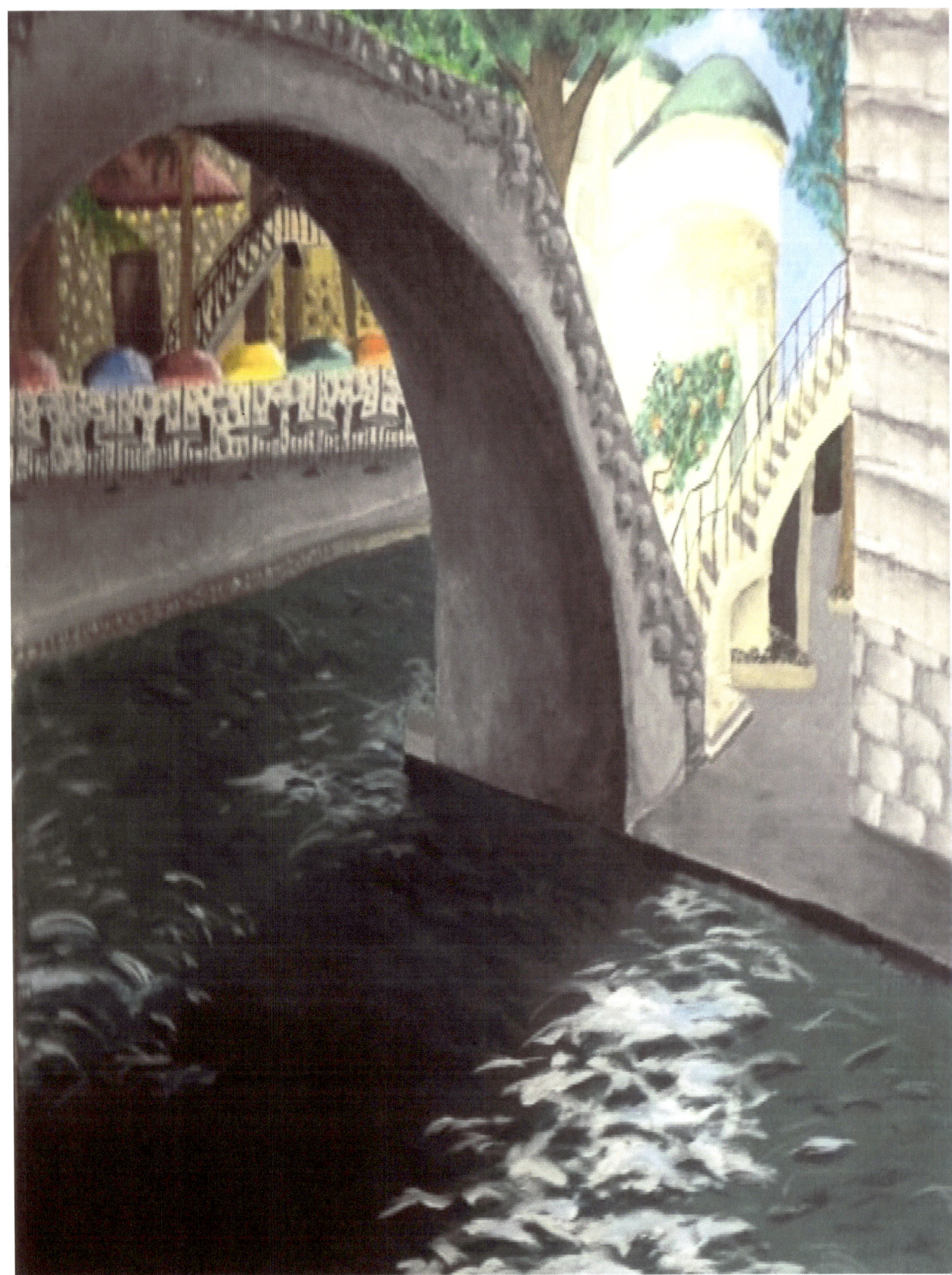

Illustrated by Kenndieie Nelson, 8

One and the Same

by Taylor Boss, 5

My best friend is my sister,

My sister is my best friend,

We'll stick together,

From beginning to end.

My sister is my best friend,

My best friend is my sister,

My best friend, my sister,

They are one and the same.

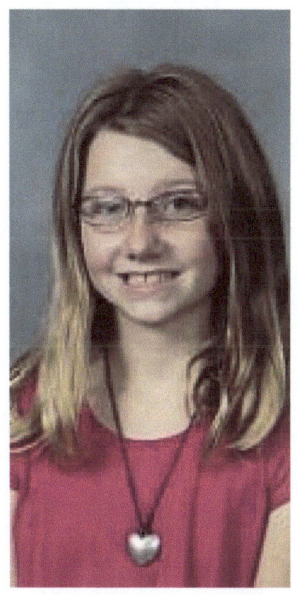

Taylor Boss, 5
Band Major

Live Your Life

by Eliza Reed, 5

Live your life.

Don't waste it.

Live it while you can.

Love you.

Believe you can.

Believe in yourself.

Have fun.

Don't worry.

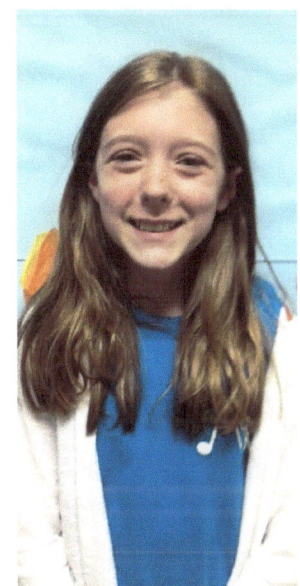

Eliza Reed, 5
Ballet Major

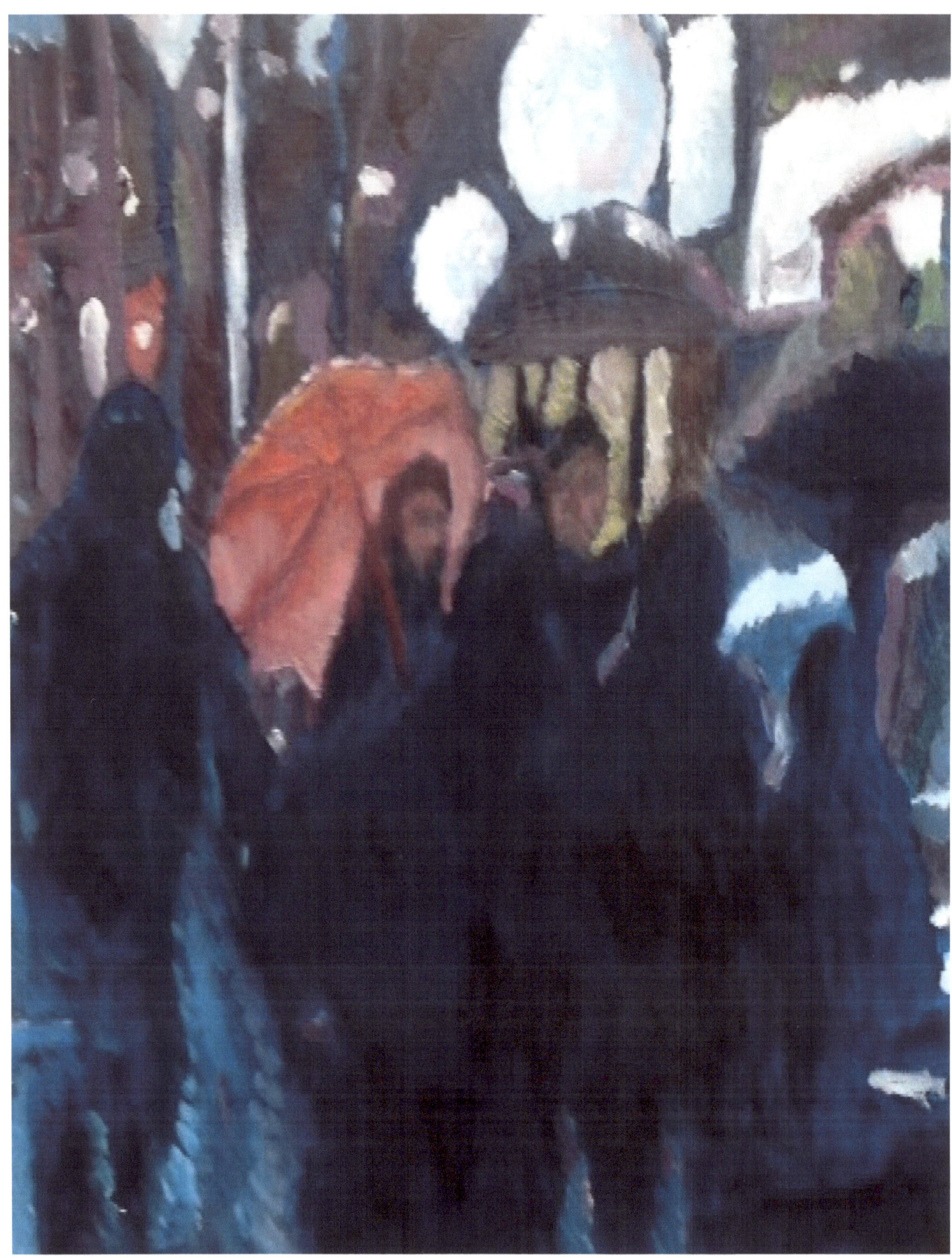

Illustrated by Michael Lozovoy, 7

Sing Your Song

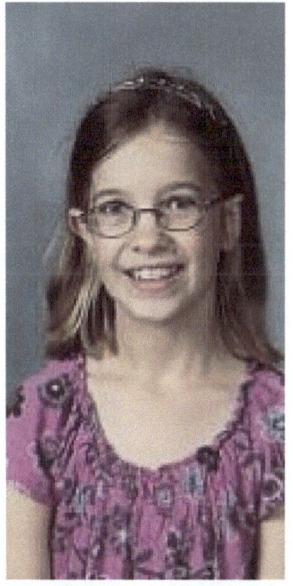

by Maren Bylund, 5

Sing your song

In the sun.

Sing out loud

Make it fun.

Sing it in the rain.

Sing it in the snow.

Sing your song

Wherever you go.

Maren Bylund, 5
Strings Major

Don't Worry

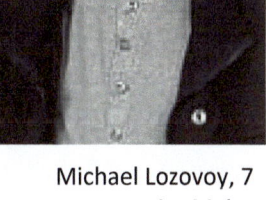

by Michael Lozovoy, 7

Don't worry. I got your back. And your spine too.

Don't worry. It's all covered. We just ran out of blankets so we started using pillows.

Don't worry. Everything's all right. We destroyed everything that was left.

Don't worry. It's no problem. Problems are all that problems are made of.

Don't worry. Things will make sense later. But for now let's just hope we get dollars.

Don't worry. Everything will be clear. Once we finish washing the windows.

Don't worry. Everything in time will get done. But right now I'm taking a break from rhymes and puns.

Michael Lozovoy, 7
Art Major

Bow to the Mirror

by Katrin Flores and Kasey Fields, 8

Katrin Flores, 8
Creative Writing Major

Kasey Fields, 8
Creative Writing Major

Bow to the mirror.

Reflections of every sickening

Flaw, every blemish,

Every bite

Of the words from the world which hides

Beneath the whirl of happy and smiles…

And plastic.

Too many words go

Without thought;

Too many battles are pointlessly fought

Because our actions come first,

And the right deed second.

The clock ticks on to

The lingering trap awaiting its prey

In which the victim's eyes may never

See another day because there

Was no other way but out.

Out of lies and excuses

Out of pain, yet plastered with

Bruises through beatings

From the idealistic image of perfection

Which must be achieved to be brought to the level of humanity

Stormy as those orbs are that stare

Back at me, weathered and tethered as

My soul might be,

Bow to the mirror.

Bogged down by unrealistic expectations;

The only goal in sight is perfection

Running

Running

Trying to get to that untouchable mark…

But tripping right before it.

Its light shines too bright,

But its beauty is transfixing.

Stumbling with foggy vision,

Good opportunities pass by-

Only perfect is visible.

The final goal must be reached

But what is failed to see a myriad of times is this:

Perfection is only dreamed of and

Cannot be touched.

Yet often missed are the tiny

Telltale cracks-

The chinks in the armor-

The ugliness that cowers

Behind a mask of beauty

Covering up its true self.

I aspire to be great,

To be loved,

To be enveloped within

One above the beast whom we see

In that reflection.

The folds of respect among others

Who are expected to be respected,

Only that

Is but a mere fantasy.

Tickled night after night

Then tucked away from the light—

Tucked away into a dream and

Separated from reality.

Every day I am reminded that

I am *not* great,

That I am *never* loved,

That I will never be acknowledged—

Just stooping profoundly beneath the mediocre;

Forever stuck in the NEVER.

Bow to the mirror.

But twinkle bright

Through the night

Help us all to find the light

That guides our path,

Leads the way

Past the fogginess of gray.

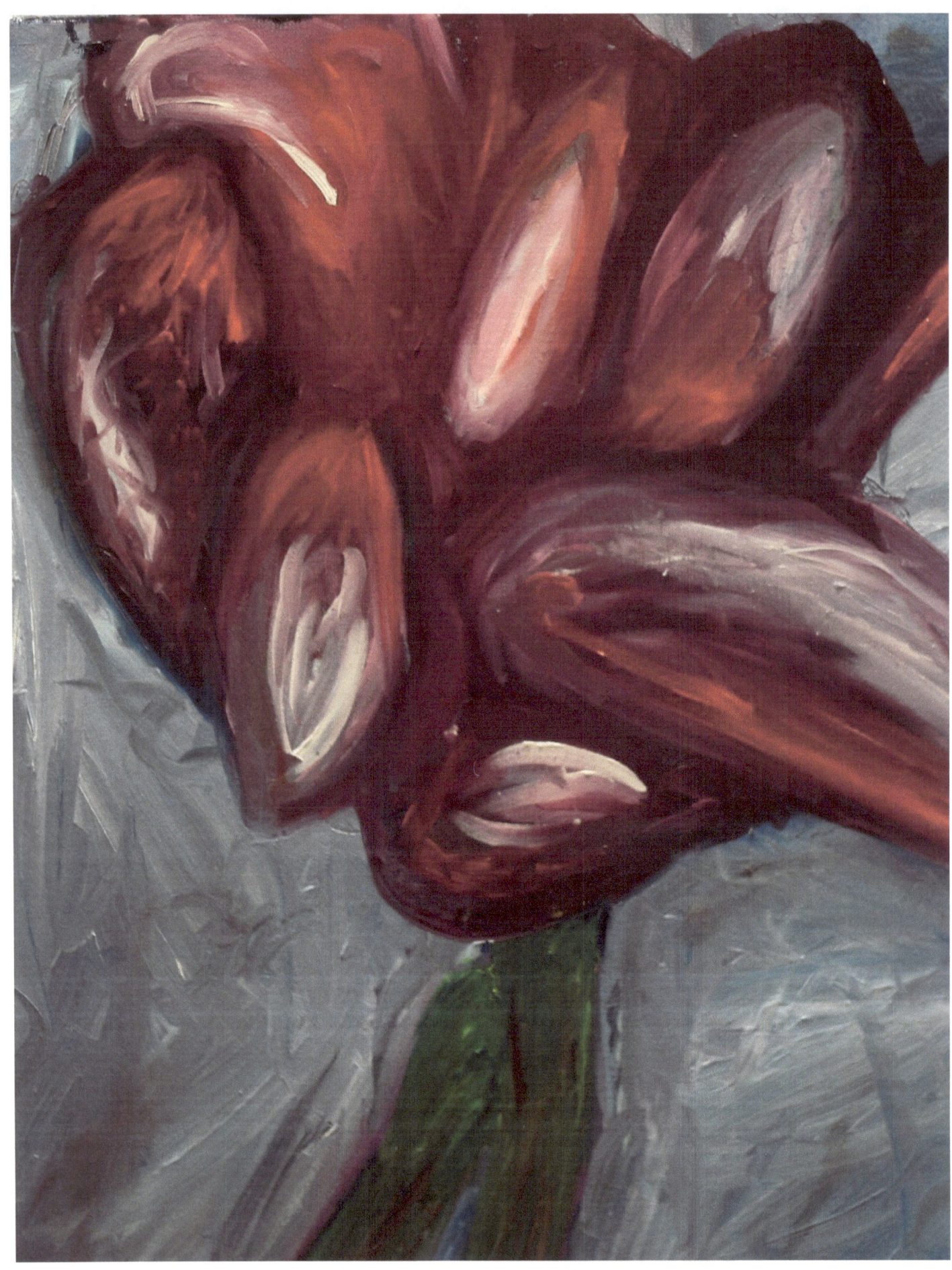

Illustrated by Jace Burt, 7

Owls at Night

by Aedon Gunn, 6

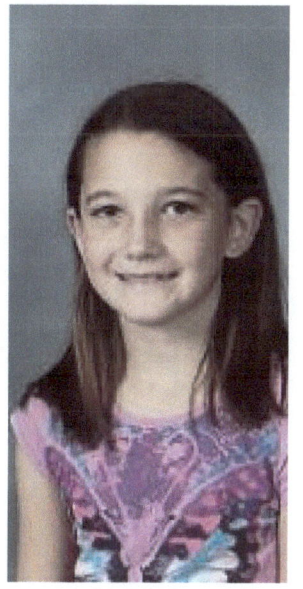

Aedon Gunn, 6
Visual Art Major

Owls swooping,

Through the midnight sky.

Listening all night,

To the baby's cry.

Scouring the ground,

For a nice treat.

Hoping to find,

Something to eat.

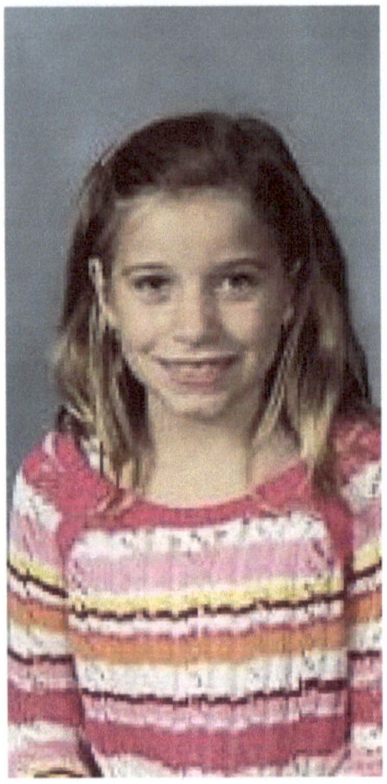

The Dream Room

by Madelyn Groth, 5

The room with the green walls

Is where we all learned to write.

It is known to the fifth graders

As where they were shown the light.

It is where ideas

Spark like lightning.

It is my

Dream room

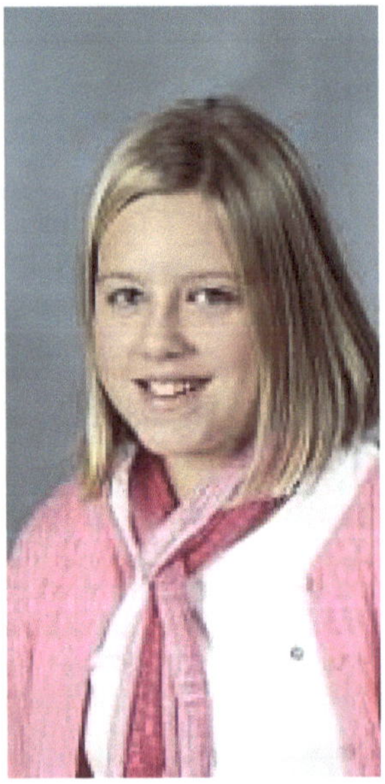

Madelyn Groth, 5
Ballet Major

Fall

by Anna Clay, 7

Trees find the rhythm of the wind,

And start to dance to its soft music.

As they sway back and forth,

Leaves jump down from the moving branches,

Landing on the soft grass below.

Then get taken away to a new future, to find a new life..

Anna Clay, 7
Creative Writing Major

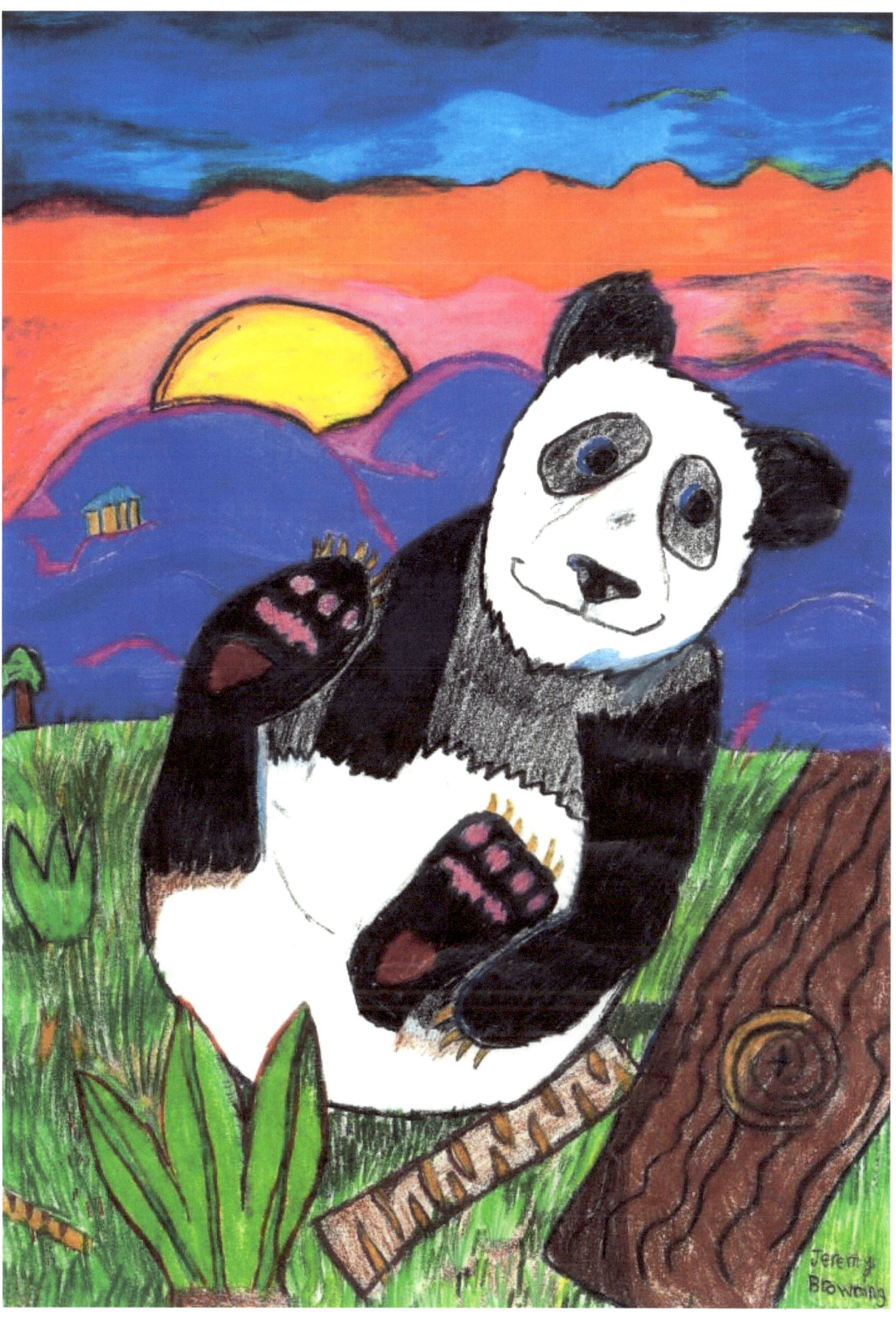

Illustrated by Jeremy Browning, 4

Fishy Friday

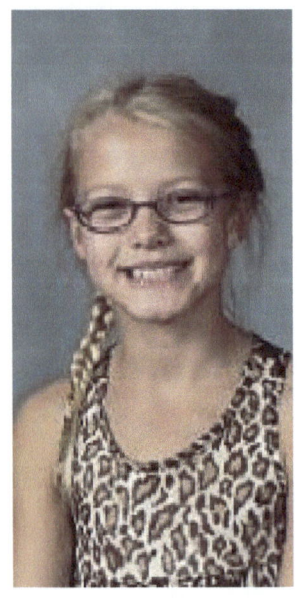

Sarah Howell, 5
Creative Writing Major

by Sarah Howell, 5

As I walked into my living room,

My pet fish went *Zoom!*

Oh, Fred, I wish that I was a little old fish like you!

But, it could never happen. I am a human!

Look at you, you little boy blue.

Why can't we switch lives?

Boom! Snap! Pop!

All of a sudden, slimy scales covered my skin.

Oh thank you, my little fish!

Well, now I have work to do!

Squish, squish, squish.

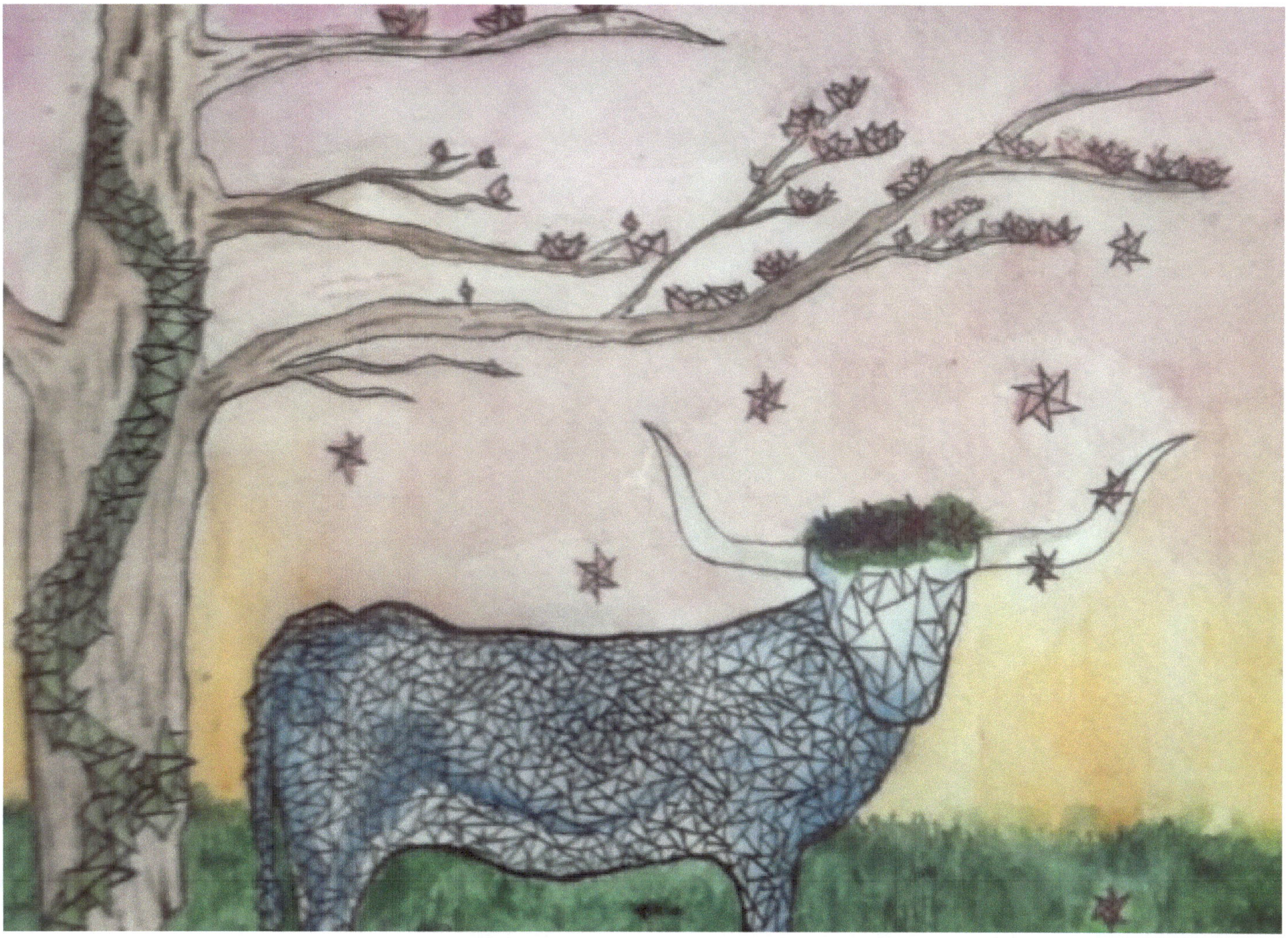

Illustrated by Allison Padilla, 6

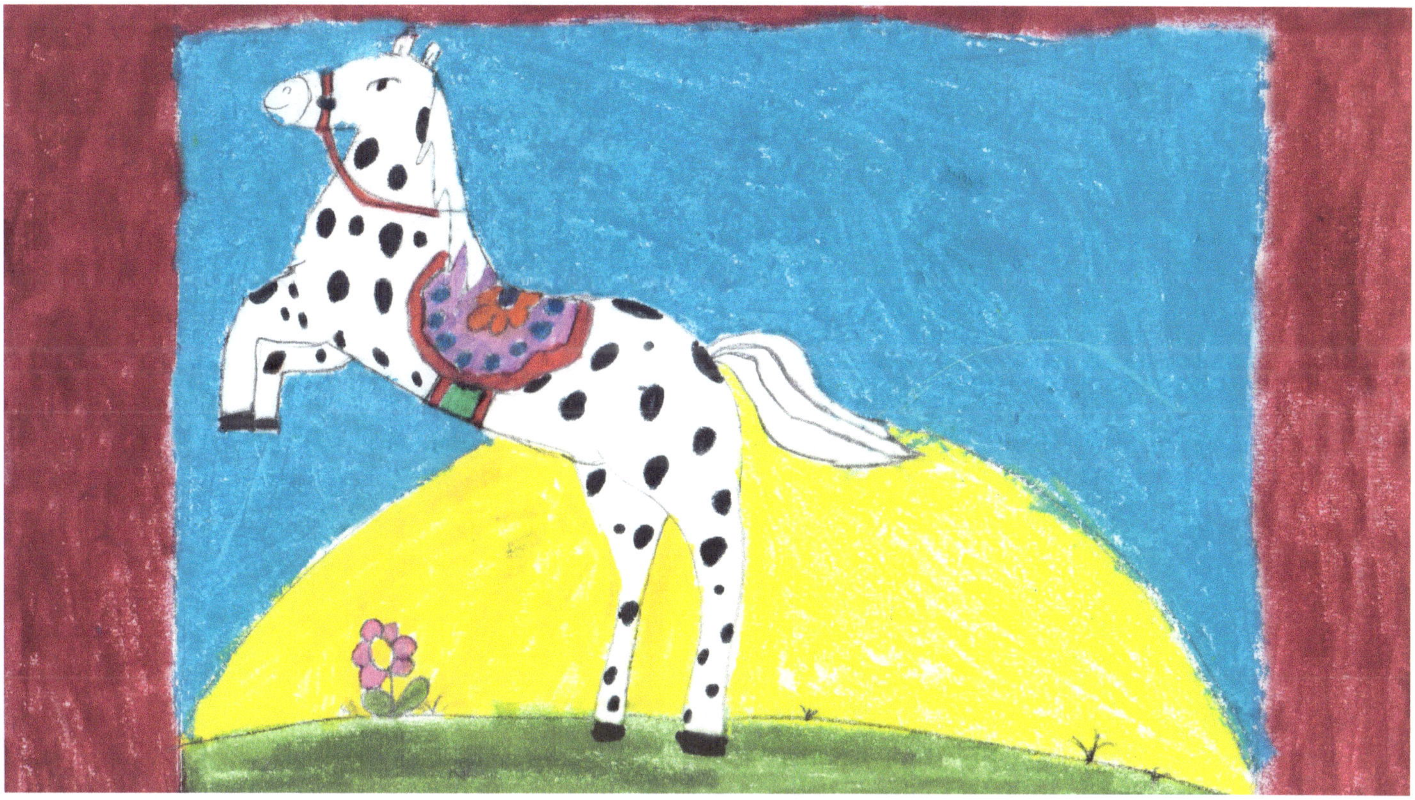

Illustrated by Kadence Ginter, 4

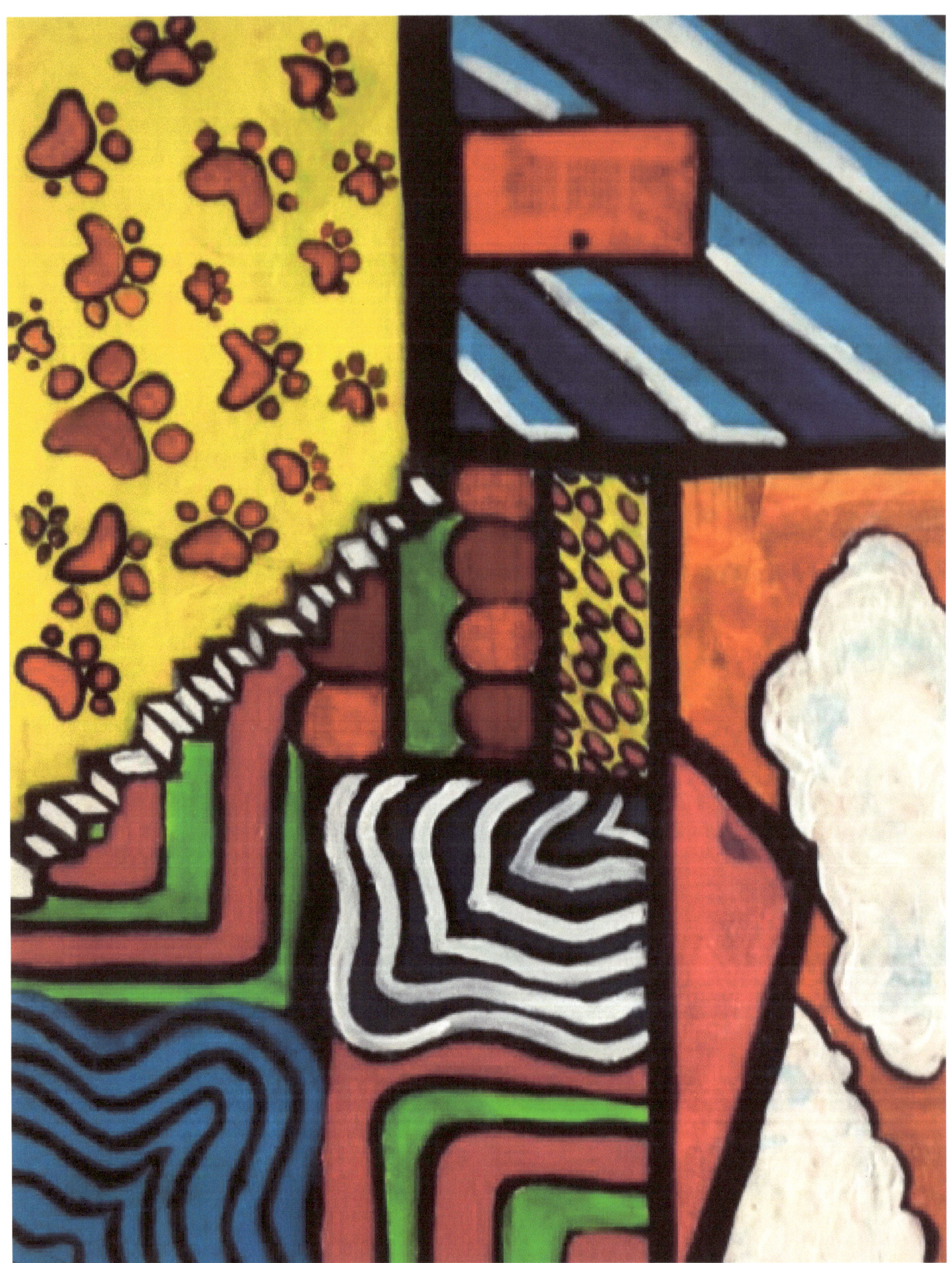

Illustrated by Landon Sarrett, 5

New York, New York

by Kennedy Cobb, 6

Whoosh! a bright yellow taxi flies by,

As all of the large, flashy billboards

Change color like the blink of an eye.

Men shout out things for sale,

As office workers practically yell into smart phones.

The smell of fast food and the sight of tall sky scrapers

Overwhelms me,

Taking in the muggy, cold, and open air mixed with exhaust.

The horns of taxis, buses, corvettes, and cars missing

bumpers boom loudly.

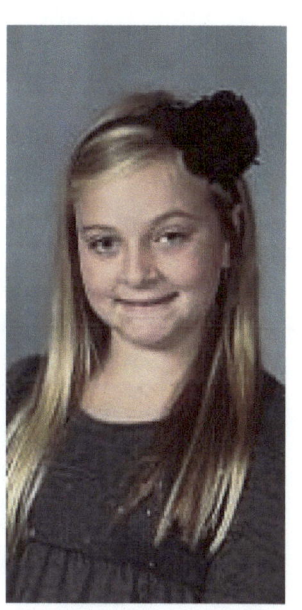

Kennedy Cobb, 6
Creative Writing Major

Homeless walk alongside the wealthy, talking with loud,

excited chatter.

And an enclosed bridge drips rain droplets, as busy people

walk across, and another large and flashy billboard blinks.

I hop on the crowded subway tram

I know I'm happy here…

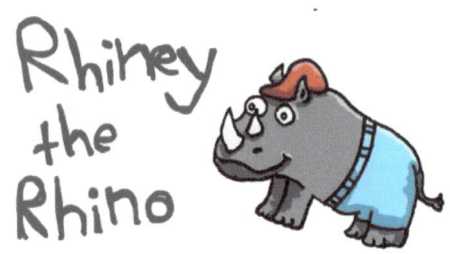

Rhiney the Rhino

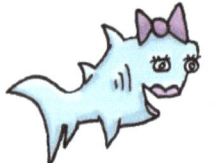

Written by Avery Logsdon

Illustrated by Michael Lozovoy

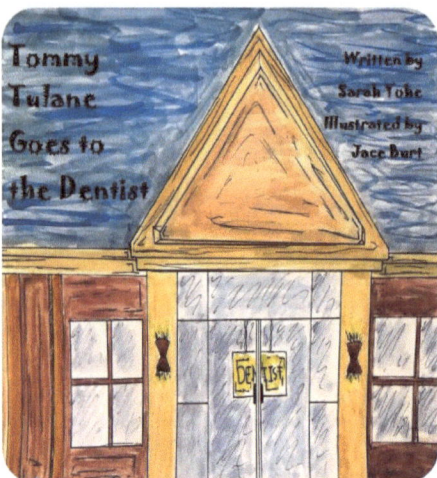

Tommy Tulane Goes to the Dentist

Written by Sarah Yoke

Illustrated by Jace Burt

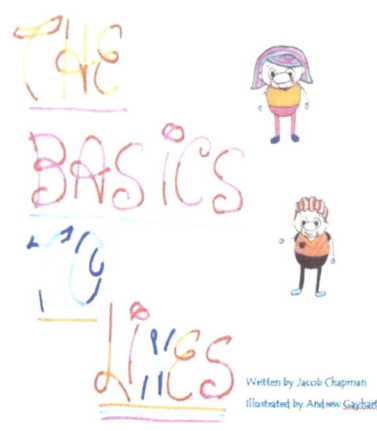

THE BASICS of my Lives

Written by Jacob Chapman

Illustrated by Andrew Gaybart

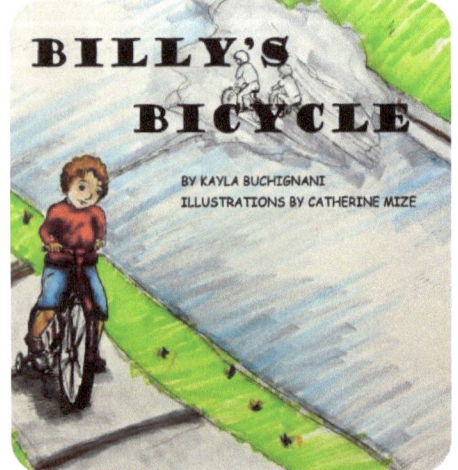

BILLY'S BICYCLE

BY KAYLA BUCHIGNANI

ILLUSTRATIONS BY CATHERINE MIZE

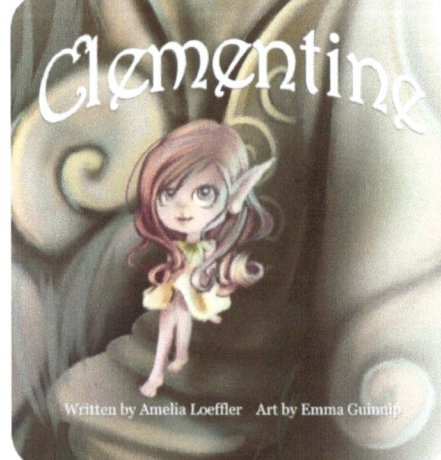

Clementine

Written by Amelia Loeffler   Art by Emma Guintip

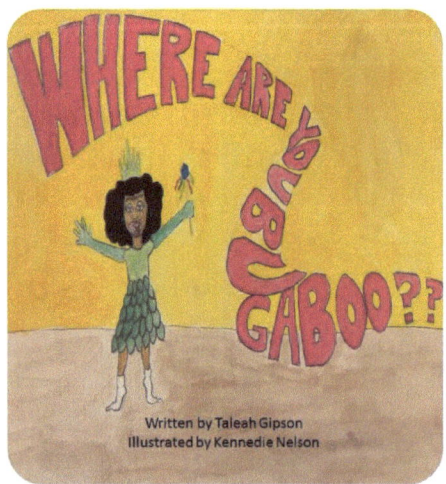

WHERE ARE YOU BUGABOO??

Written by Taleah Gipson

Illustrated by Kennedie Nelson

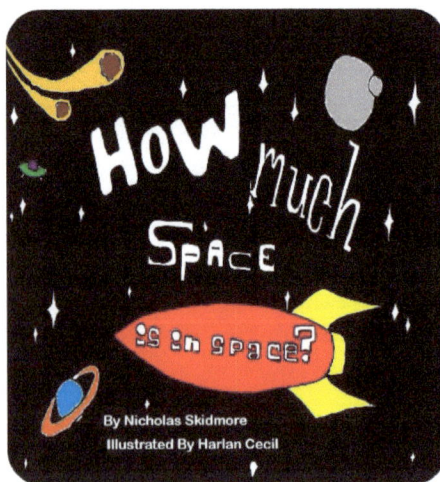

HOW much SPACE is in space?

By Nicholas Skidmore

Illustrated By Harlan Cecil

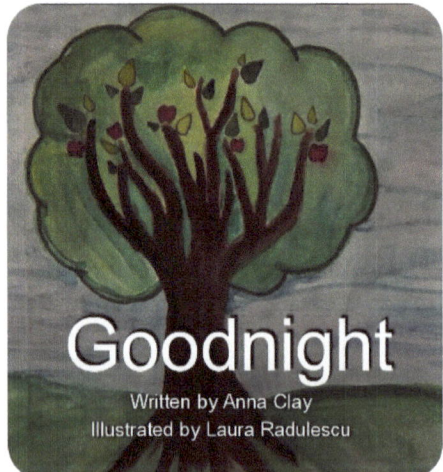

Goodnight

Written by Anna Clay

Illustrated by Laura Radulescu

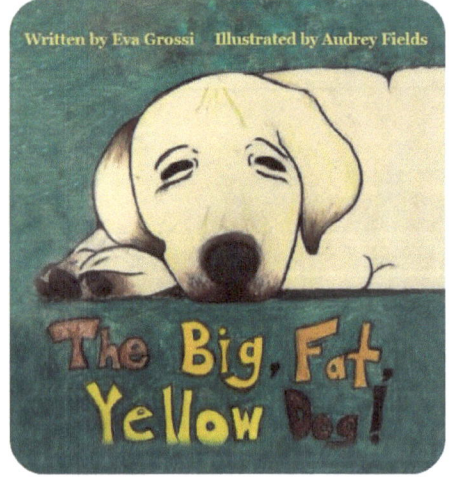

Written by Eva Grossi   Illustrated by Audrey Fields

The Big, Fat, Yellow Dog!

Wilbert Gets a Job

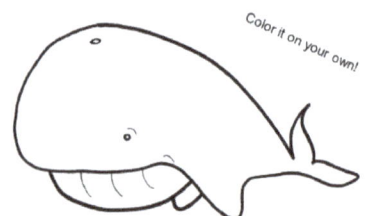

Color it on your own!

Written by Nathan Pennington

Illustrated by Anna Gilligan

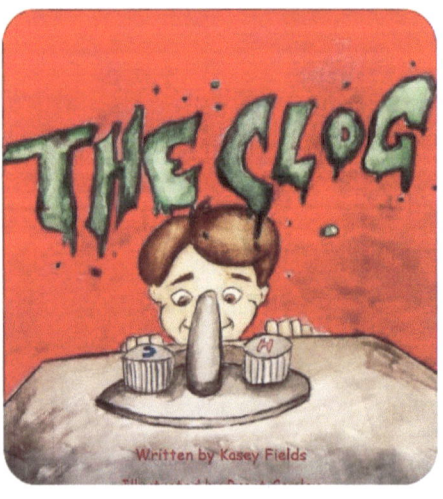

THE CLOG

Written by Kasey Fields

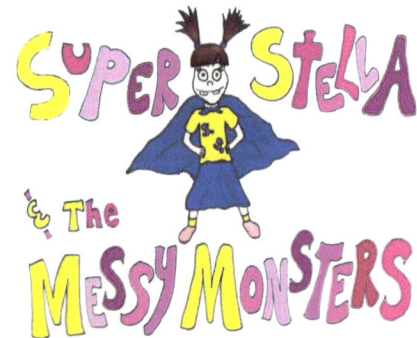

SUPER STELLA & THE MESSY MONSTERS

Written by

Katrin Flores

Illustrated by

John Clark Baker

Illustrated Children's Book Project (Collaboration between Middle School Creative Writing and Visual Art Majors)

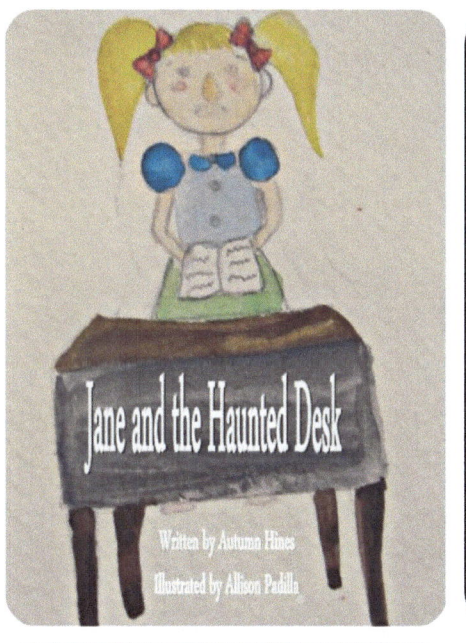

Jane and the Haunted Desk

Written by Autumn Hines

Illustrated by Allison Padilla

Connor and Cody

Written and Illustrated by John Giuliani

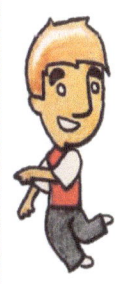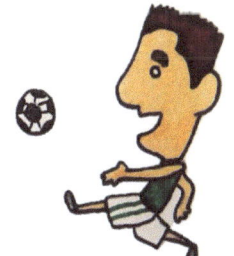

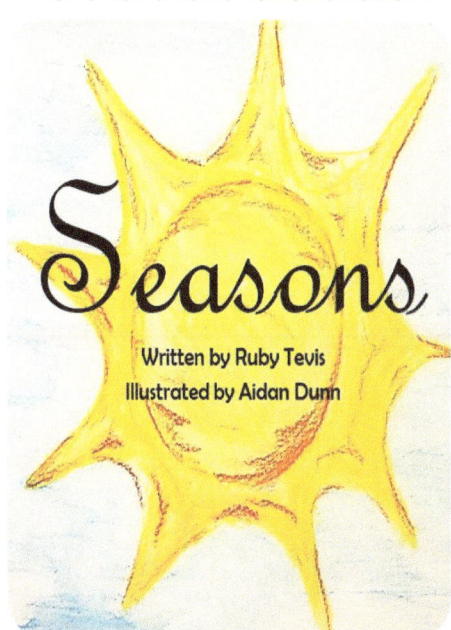

Seasons

Written by Ruby Tevis

Illustrated by Aidan Dunn

Pajama Day Jam

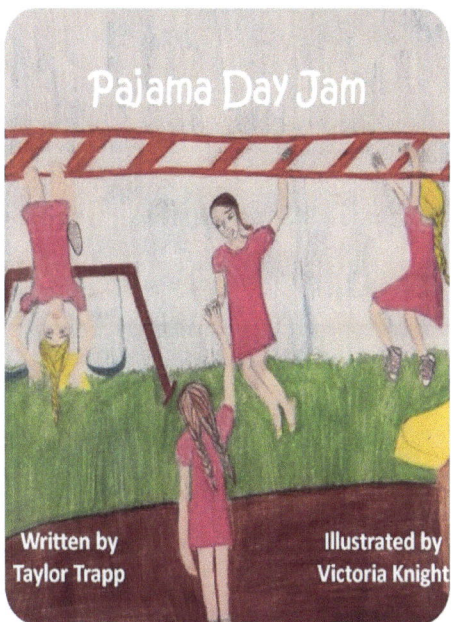

Written by
Taylor Trapp

Illustrated by
Victoria Knight

Brooklyn Vs. Vegetables

Written by Jahnavi Stivers

Illustrated by Lexi Ocampo

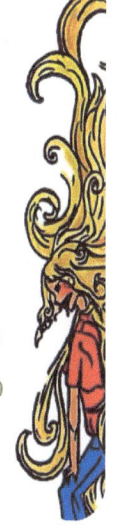

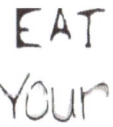

EAT Your VEGETABLES

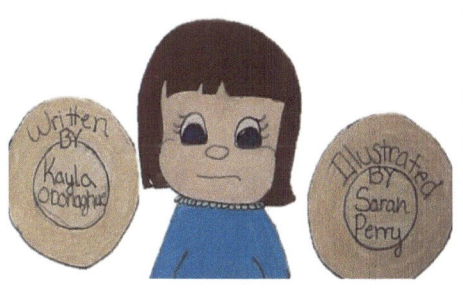

Written By Kayla O'Donaghue

Illustrated BY Sarah Perry

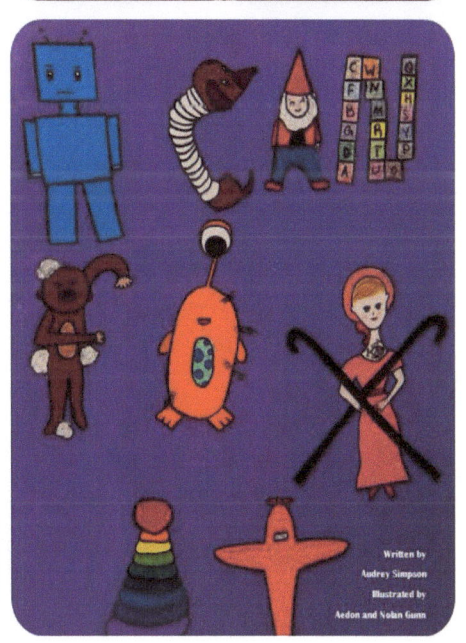

Written by
Audrey Simpson

Illustrated by
Aedon and Nolan Gunn

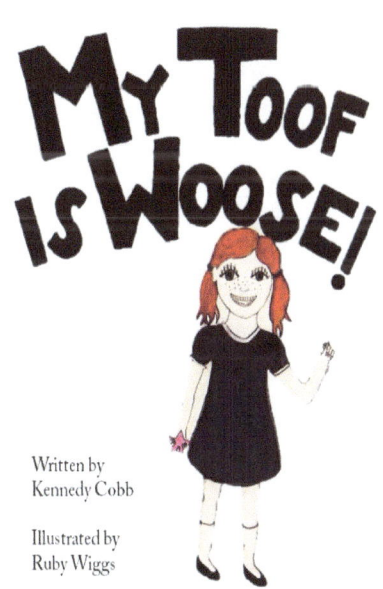

MY TOOF IS WOOSE!

Written by
Kennedy Cobb

Illustrated by
Ruby Wiggs

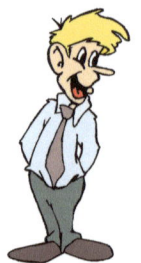 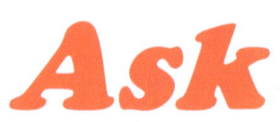

Q: Dear Smitty, why are The Beatles so bad?

A: Well, a wise man once said that The Beatles are an acquired taste; if you don't like them, acquire some taste.

Q: What is the best juice to drink on the third of October, during a waxing crescent moon, with your hands tied behind your back?

A: Well, you would have to clarify whether or not you are sporting a handle bar mustache. If so, Apple. However, if not, I would simply advise water.

Q: Why is it always so cold in Mrs. Hardy's room?

A: Yes.

Q: Dear Smitty, can you help me with my face?   Sincerely, Nathan Pennington

A: I'm not a miracle worker, honey.

Q: We are delighted that you have joined Pandora. Welcome! Pandora was founded by musicians and music-lovers and it has been a labor of love for us for more than ten years. A decade into this journey it continues to thrill us each time someone new chooses to make Pandora part of their day.

A: What's your question?

Q: You know, sometimes I think about my life and what it would be like if I lived somewhere else. Or if I lived the American Dream, or maybe I'm already living the American Dream and I just don't know it, maybe somewhere out in space there is a giant duck watching over us and using floating tropical islands to defend the Earth from asteroids. And if such a duck guardian does exist then what would life without it be like? Would it result in a catastrophe like the "Life as we knew it" book series (which I have not read)? I would appreciate it if Ask Smitty could answer every single one of the preceding questions for me. XOXOXOXOXOXO

A: Ain't nobody got time for that.

Q: Hey I have problems with my hair.   -Sincerely, John Giuliani

A: Be quiet, John.

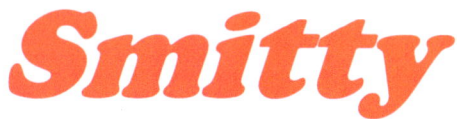

Q: I like Windows, but my friend is more of a Dell fan. What's your favorite type of computer?

A: What is a computer?

Q: Who is your favorite actor in the movie Casablanca?

A: Humphrey Bogart.

Q: What is the square root of -253,494,620 multiplied by 87,732,991 divided by PI ?

A: -7.0791613e+15. Do the math.

Q: There are billions and billions of people in the world. Do you think that you matter? I will go ahead and answer that for you. No you don't. Ha-ha, sucker.

A: Well, thanks for dampening my spirits.

Q: What is your favorite dressing on your salad?

A: The blood of my enemies.

Q: I have trouble seeing at night. Can you buy me a night light?   -Sincerely, Walker Cody

A: Huh-huh, yeah.

Q: K-mart stinks.

A: Haters gonna hate.

Q: There are people who don't trust me. This is bothering me, because I want them to. What can I do to get them to trust me?

A: Just show them that you are so dedicated to earn their trust that you actually sent a real question to Ask Smitty. Also, buy them an edition of Literature and Art magazine, so that when they read Ask Smitty, they will realize that they are being referenced in this question. So, if you have a friend who you don't trust, and he/she bought you an issue of Literature and Art magazine, then you should trust him/her.

4th Grade Biopoems

Osar

Tall, smart, interesting, awesome

Son of Susan Larson

Lover of Mom, Dad, and Milou

Who feels happy, excited, and tired

Who needs a violin, computer, and love

Who gives violin performances, hugs, love

Who fears stitches, spiders, and tornados

Who would like to see China, Russia, and

India

Heft

Jeremy

Creative, kind, carefree, calm

Brother of Christopher

Lover of animals, fantasy, and his cousins

Who feels coolheaded about acting,

Inspired by art, and comfortable reading

Who needs a good book, drawing paper and

Pencil, and dark chocolate

Who gives art, Happiness, and love when

Others need it most

Who fears a world with more violence, a

world without books, and losing another

cousin

Who would like to see London, his art in a

museum, and the Himalayan mountains

Browning

Luke

Nice, smart, creative, silly

Friend of Jeremy

Lover of gaming, Legos, and music

Who feels tired, sad, and frightened

When needs more game systems, a new apple

computer, video games, and stuffed animals

Who fears spiders, insects, and cicadas

Who would like to see Lego land, Disney

Land, and the 2014 Comic Con

Nuzzo

5th Grade Six Word Memoirs

Want dog. Love dog. Never will.

I was lazy, now I'm exhausted.

Here one minute, gone the next.

Life is learning, laughing, and happiness .

I have never discovered Platform 9 3/4.

Once a plucker now a player.

2013-2014 Literature and Art Magazine Staff

Interested in joining the Literature and Art Magazine Staff for next year? Check out what each peer elected position entails.

Editor in Chief: Buchignani, Kayla

Management

Delegate who receives what jobs, who writes on which subjects, and who provides discipline and motivates the staff. The editor in chief is responsible for overseeing and managing the rest of the staff members who produce and edit content. Some tasks within management might be delegated to editors as the editor in chief sees fit.

Research

Key parts of the job include keeping tabs on customer and market response to content as well as monitoring the publication's position among competitors. The editor is chief is responsible for monitoring competing magazines' content and success. Strategic planning and solving problems based on the research are also part of the job.

Editing Skills

Maintaining the company's standards of excellence, the publication's format and its image are important job objectives for the editor in chief. This top editor will check the copy for errors and make light and heavy editing decisions as needed. Previously edited copy comes to the editor in chief last as a final check before publication. Attention to detail is key for this part of the job. While these tasks are sometimes delegated to other employees, the editor in chief is the one who is ultimately responsible.

Referencing

Verify all quotes or citations of previously published works as accurate and correctly referenced. An editor in chief serves as the final fact checker for all referenced portions of the work being published. In larger companies, the editor in chief might delegate these responsibilities to researchers, editors or copy editors.

Completion

Editors in chief at newspapers and magazines ensure that the entire publication is properly laid out and full by conducting a final review before sending the publication to print.

Assistant Editor: Grossi, Eva

Assist Editor in Chief with all above duties.

Poetry Editors: Clay, Anna; Gipson, Taleah; Knight, Victoria; Comely, Brent

Compile, then read, edit, and revise submitted poems. Assist if necessary with poem layout in the magazine.

Nonfiction/Academic Editors: Male, Serena; Webster, Ella; Guinnip, Emma

Acquire, then proofread and revise any nonfiction/academic submissions including creative nonfiction, personal essays, lyric essays, memoirs, and literary journalism. Assist if necessary with nonfiction layout in the magazine.

Feature Editors: Stivers, Jahnavi; Trapp, Taylor; Logsdon, Avery; Male, Serena

Acquire, then proofread and revise any short stories, flash fiction, graphic novels, self-contained novel excerpts, and plays. Assist if necessary with feature layout in the magazine.

Art and Photography Editors: Connelly, Olivia; Fields, Audrey; Gilligan, Anna; Knight, Victoria

Compile photographs and artwork for the magazine, then color correct in Photoshop as needed. Assist if necessary with art and photography layout in the magazine.

Designers: Gilligan, Anna; Tonks, Benjamin;' Burt, Jace

Meet with editors to coordinate the appearance of their upcoming issue. Occasionally, magazine designers also work with photographers gathering ideas on the best way to present their work. Designers decide on and create things such as typefaces and fonts for the magazine's cover and headlines, as well as which type of artwork will be used with each story, and how the two elements will best be tied together. They also design the all-important "flag," or the title of the magazine that appears at the top of each issue and acts as the publication's trademark or logo.

Submission-Narrowers: Logsdon, Avery; Naish, Michael; Resultay, BJ; Ryzowicz, Jonathan

Promote the magazine, work to gain submissions, publicize, complete "odd jobs," and narrow down when submissions are large in number. Help other areas as needed.

Advisor: Andrea Stang

All students worked on the Weekly Beat, our newsletter.

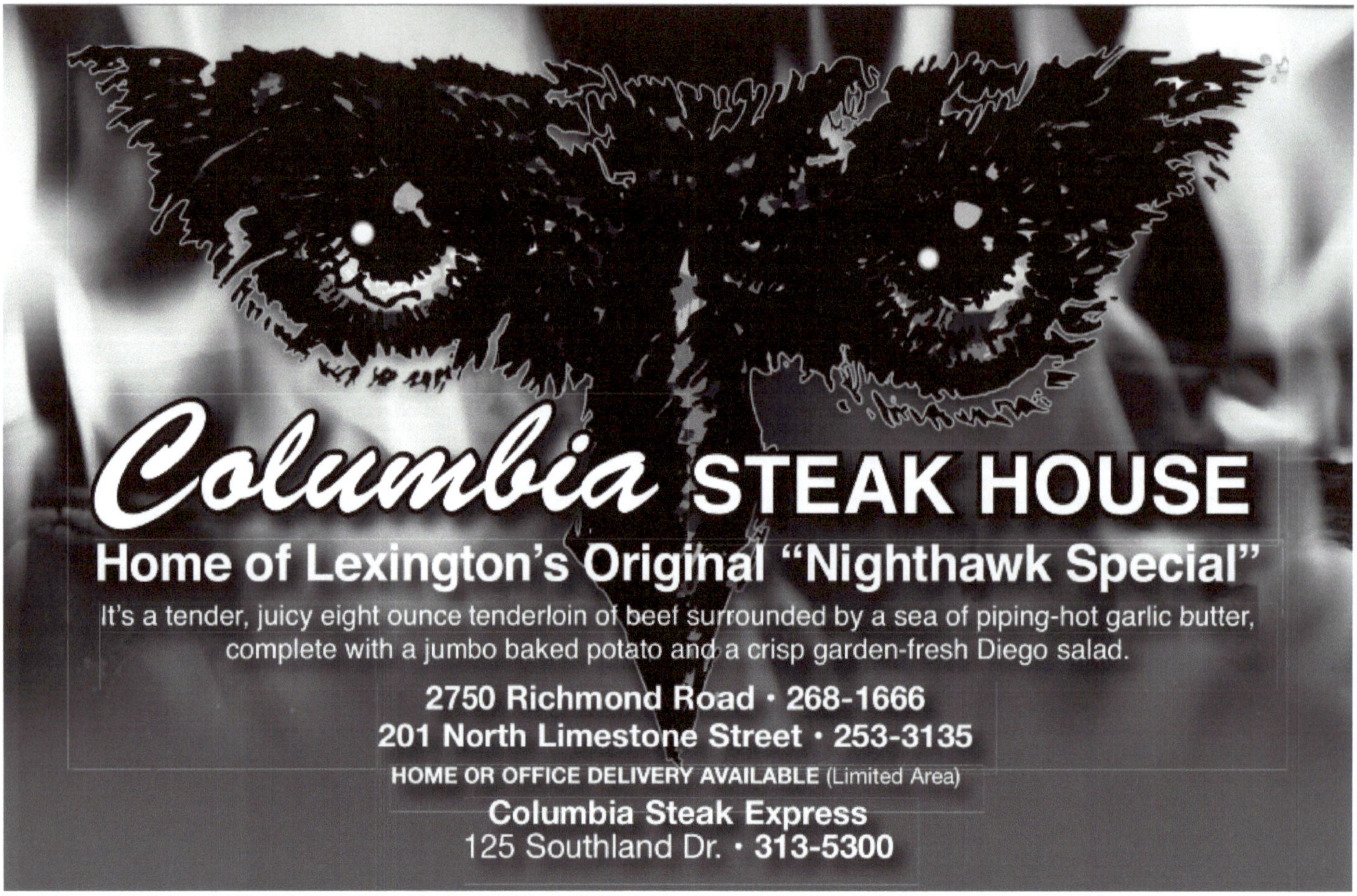

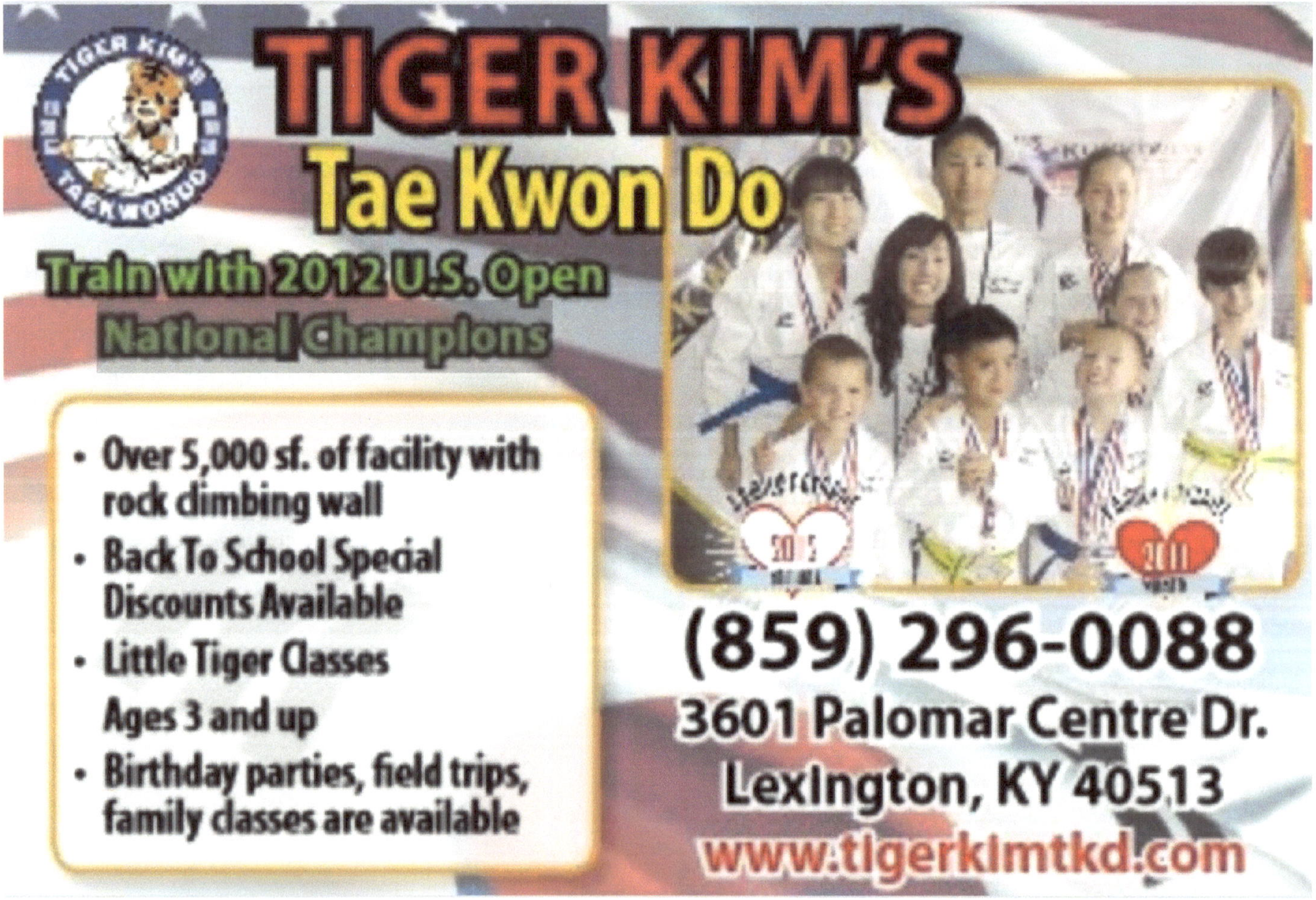

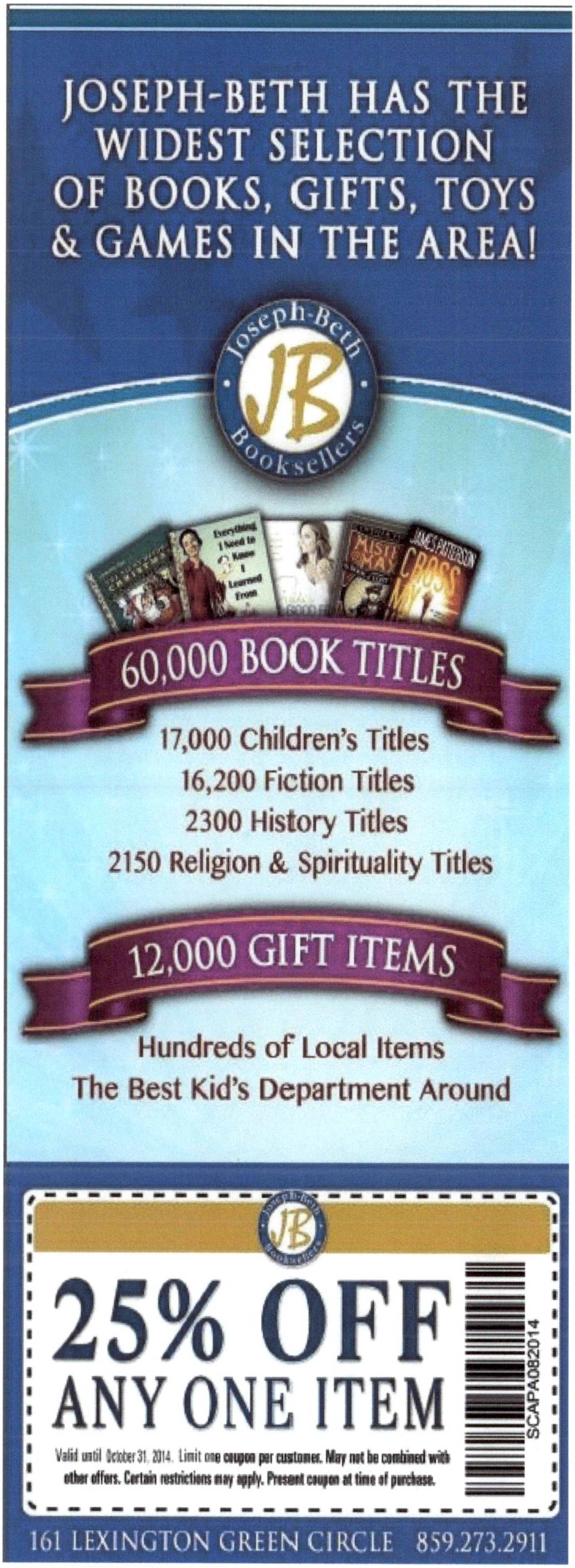

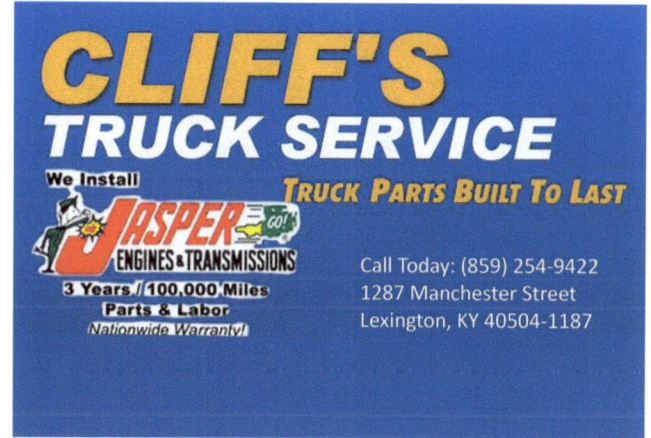

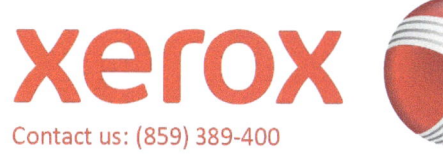
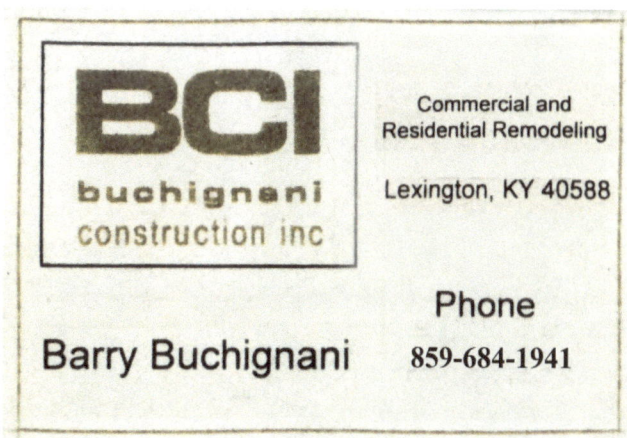

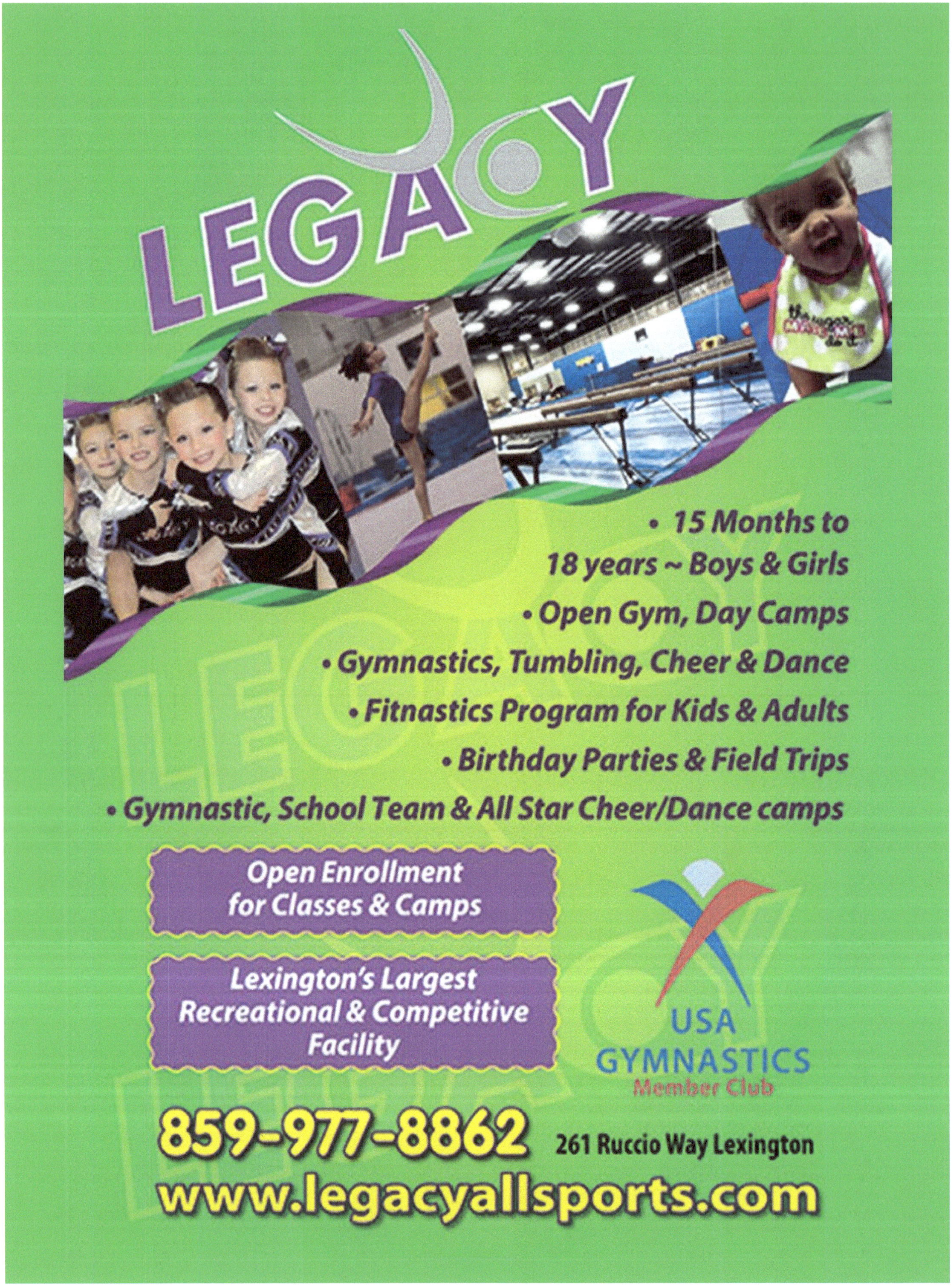

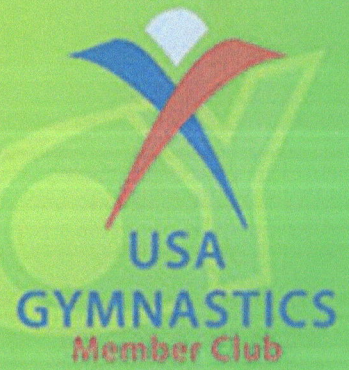

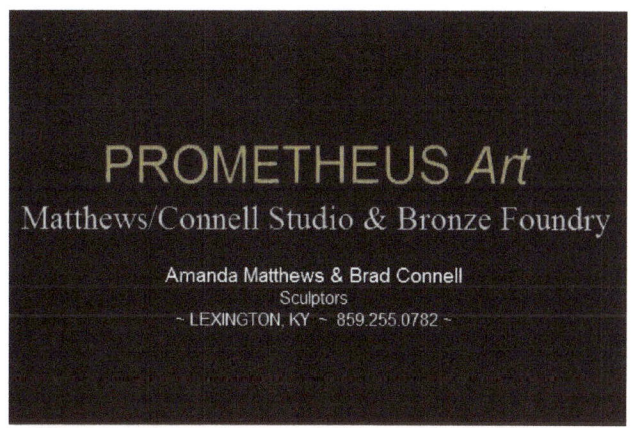
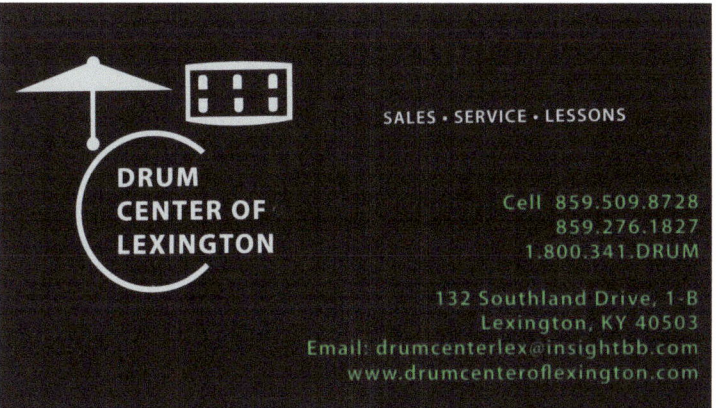
Want to be in the next Literary and Art Magazine?

Below you'll find our publication guidelines.

- **FICTION, POETRY, AND NONFICTION** We will publish short stories, flash fiction, graphic novels, self-contained novel excerpts, and plays (page number limit); poetry of all kinds, including verse plays; and all manner of creative nonfiction, including personal essays, lyric essays, memoirs, and literary journalism.

- **REVIEWS** We will publish short reviews of books (fiction and nonfiction), book-length poetry, dance/theater productions, music, art shows, locally produced movies, etc.

- **INTERVIEWS** We will publish interviews with local writers of fiction, poetry, and nonfiction, as well as dance professionals, musicians, artists, actors, etc. We also want to hear from SCAPA students about their art.

- **ARTWORK** We will publish original artwork in the form of photographs, scanned drawings, and photographed paintings, fused glass, jewelry, sculptures, pottery, metal arts, weaving, printmaking, woodcarvings, comics, etc.

Visit Mrs. Stang's website at https://blogs.fcps.net/astang to digitally submit.